Symphonies of Life

Symphonies of Life

A Collection of Poems

EMAN ABID

PARTRIDGE

A Penguin Random House Company

Print information available on the last page.

To order additional copies of this book, contact
Toll Free 800 101 2657 (Singapore)
Toll Free 1 800 81 7340 (Malaysia)
orders.singapore@partridgepublishing.com

www.partridgepublishing.com/singapore

Contents

Author's Page..9

Thank You Note... 11

Dedication 13

Symphonies of Life 15

Mind..20

Rain 22

Some 23

Free 27

Watch 28

Fashion 30

No Promises...34

Keep Looking for Winter 44

Symphony of a Warrior's Heart 46

Stop...47

Wings 49

The Road to Heaven 51

Still 53

Don't Go..54

Past, Present, and Future 56

Bulb 57

Happiness 60

Game 62

Lost..65

Security...66

Treasure 67

My Space 68

Dear Mother 69

Dreams 78

Plan..79

Regrets 81

Time 82

Free Fall 84

Part 87

Not Every Question 89

Sweets and Candies 90

Where?..91

Stage 92

Fear...93

Beauty...95

A Business World 96

Poison 97

Roses...99

Hope... 101

Drowning..102

Sacrifice 103

Wind...105

Facts..107

Dear Dad 108

Laughter 114

Woman 120

Change 121

Healing 123

Rush 125

Doubts 126

Road 127

Same 129

Control 130

The End? Or the Beginning? 132

Greed 133

Stars 134

Sugar 135

The Elusive Search for Words 136

Dreams of Grandeur 137

Pain 139

Joy 143

End 144

Lies Are Day; Truth Is night 146

Hide 147

Dear Brother 149

Face It All 153

Desperation 154

Forgiveness 155

Slow 158

Hunger 159

Stay with Me 160

Promises 162

Victory 164

Masquerade 165

Poverty 166

Afraid 167

Do You Have What It Takes? 168

Memories 171

Tell Me 173

Don't Look Back 176

Passion 177

Thread 178

A Perfect Day 179

Ice 180

Fire 182

Swept Away 184

Home 186

Where I Belong … 191

About the Author 193

About the Book 195

End Notes 197

Author's Page

Eman Abid has been writing since she was 8 years old. She wrote her first poem 'Mother' at the age of 10, and completed her first novel at 12. After graduating from The International School of Choueifat-Dubai, she was awarded a scholarship from Sorbonne University. However, in order to concentrate on her writing, Eman Abid stayed in Dubai. She achieved a degree in Business Management from The American University in Dubai (AUD) along with a certificate of Cinema Director and Line Producer from The Hollywood Film Institute from Dubai as well. Currently, Eman is working on Symphonies of life, a collection of poems 2nd edition, and getting her novels and short stories ready for publication.

Some of her upcoming novels include a series of books based around a young man's journey into a world he cannot understand, yet cannot escape.

The titles for the series are as thus:

Road to Dynasty
Under the bridge
No exit
My way or the highway

Some other novels include the following titles:

Shadow
The Violin player

Thank You Note

I would like to begin by thanking God for all that He has given me. I would also like to thank my family, especially my mother. I wouldn't be a writer today, or even a decent human being if it hadn't been for my family's love, support and guidance. To have any one of those things is an asset. To have all three is a blessing. I'd also like to thank my friends who have always been there for me.

A special thank you for Dr. Sandra Alexander and Mr. Cory Lowell Grewell Ph.D. for dedicating their precious time reviewing and proofreading this book. A special thank you for Ms. Alice Johnson as well for dedicating her valuable time proofreading my extended poems.

There are so many more people I haven't quite mentioned here. What can I say? They are playing the music, and it's time for me to exit this proverbial stage. Or in other words, I have run out of page.

With Love,
Eman Abid

Dedication

I dedicate this book to my family.

My mother, father and my brother Suhaib

Symphonies of Life

'A poet is, before anything else, a person who is passionately
in love with language.'

- W. H. Auden

The work of Eman Abid is replete with the language of hopefulness, aspiration and wonder, and with an obvious love for the endless possibilities of life itself. It has been said that all philosophy begins in wonder and thus, much of Eman's work has a truly philosophical quality. The subjects of the mind, the heart, fear, life's very purpose, and a myriad of other unfathomable human experiences all find expression in her poems. Whether considering the connections between time and the secrets of life in *Wind,* or the differences between the courageous and the weak in *Some,* her work takes everyday human experiences and observations and shows them in their truest, most meaningful aspects. As we find in the poem *No Promises,* hers is a world about the paradoxical liberation and difficulty of devotion. Hers is a world where the mundane objects of life come alive, as we find in the poem *Bulb* – a piece that conveys the humility of the mundane and the overlooked. Hers is poetry about decision making and about the struggle to become 'fully oneself' in a world where half-heartedness often gets one by. The poem *The Road to Heaven* abounds with references to our daily challenge to 'do good' and 'do no harm', and a warning that although life is a gift, it is also a test. Hers is a world, as seen in *Symphony of a Warrior's Heart,* where love and peace are met by obligation. Her work is, indeed, about the symphonies of life composed every day, by the high-born and the humble of this world. Each human composition is made of moments of deep contemplation, times of simple pleasure, or points where we find ourselves between a rock and hard place. These very moments are the stuff of life, and Eman's work brings us into the midst of it and shows us the subtle, transformative power of philosophic observation.

Sandra K. Alexander
American University in Dubai
Dubai, United Arab Emirates
August 2013

Eman Abid's poems achieve something not much poetry written in English in recent years does: they are very, very readable. It would be silly to call a book of poetry a page turner, but I find myself, upon finishing one of these poems, wanting to go on to the next one.

Abid's rhythms and use of rhyme – both internal and end rhyme – give these poems a very contemporary sound, and yet at the same point the diction, the figures and symbolism, and the deep moral tones impart an undercurrent of aesthetic wisdom that ties this poem to a poetic tradition that goes back years and years. Poems like "Some" and "Freefall", for example, illustrate the easy conversational parallelism of nascent urban oral poetry, while poems like "The Road to Heaven" impart to us in a new vernacular the proverbial wisdom of ages past. When reading Abid, I hear echoes of both the Russell Simmons Def Poetry Jam and Rumi.

Another thing that Eman Abid does in this volume, and again something poetry in English has not done nearly so well, in my estimation, for some time is speak coherently and meaningfully to her culture. The poem "Fashion," for example, asks us to think complexly about the morality of fashion, and the approach is not the simple, clichéd denunciation of materialism we might expect. There is room for the morals of aesthetics, and the whole ethical context is grounded in the extremely complex moral universe that is the contemporary city. This volume contains many poems that tackle similar instantiations of modernization, and in my mind, this is perhaps her signature contribution to both contemporary poetry in English and to twenty-first century culture.

To me, Eman Abid's poetic images and morals show the marks of being formed in the crucible of the emerging city of Dubai, the textbook instance of rapid modernization and globalization, and she wonderfully engages the challenges to traditional regional mores and ways of life that the city presents. Many of these poems have implications well beyond Dubai for modern societies that have moved so far from their roots, but only Dubai, a city whose rise to ultra-modernism and economic wealth has happened so rapidly, could give birth to the rich juxtaposition of the deep traditionalism and chic couture of our Eman Abid's poetry. Her poems are truly a monument to the region and one of the region's richer gifts of culture to the world.

Cory Lowell Grewell, Ph.D.
Assistant Professor of English
American University in Dubai

MIND

I take a stroll through my mind,
Anxious about what I may encounter, may find.
I linger on and face my fears.
They are wrong, and there's no need for tears.
I move on and face my doubts.
They are insubstantial and without cause.
Losing them would not be an important loss.
Finally I face my dreams.
They are so real – so tangible they are almost believable,
So strong they are still salvageable.
I move on from dream to dream,
My journey so smooth I could be drifting through butter, through cream.
The sky is so near;
The water is so clear;
It seems too real.
There are no what-ifs here, no second doubts.
We are who we are. Nobody touts.
In our minds, what we think is always thought to be right,
Just as the night is dark and the day is vivid and bright.
Nothing seems heavy; everything is buoyant and light.
It is easier to see beyond the light, the dark:
Clearly the difference between the two is stark.
In our minds, there's no burden,

No responsibilities.

We seek answers to unasked questions,

Ponder countless possibilities.

The gravity of reality is what pulls us back down

Into this world where no one knows what the future brings.

Once we've departed from the landscape of our minds,

We can no longer fly without wings.

In my mind, I'm free,

But in this reality I'm much like a tree –

My roots so deep down I cannot break free.

But isn't that the point? That we must stay grounded?

Anchored to a world that is real, that exists,

Not a world where imagination persists?

RAIN

Drops of my world fall on me,

Cleaning my conscience, leaving it pristine.

Then why do I feel so lost, so shattered?

Like I've made a mess of everything that ever mattered!

Drops of my world fall on me,

Leaving me clean, but tattered.

My world feels so wrong, so right,

I can now see rays of light in this dark, shadowy night.

I know I will continue to fight.

I think I'll be fine; it can't be too late.

Maybe tomorrow I can start with a clean slate?

Drops of my world fall on me, washing away my past.

Drops of my world fall on me. Nothing seems to last.

Drops of my world fall on me,

As I brace for a future both exhilarating and vast.

SOME

Some are free to walk;
Some simply enter without a knock.
Some are free to steal, to break a lock;
Some work against the clock;
Some just stand there and mock.
Some are free to judge.
Some refuse to budge.
Some always need a little nudge.
Some hold on to a grudge.
Some have given up on life's mystery.
Some just don't learn, and repeat old history.
Some always fight;
Some have never seen the light;
Some hold on too tight.
Some hide during the day, and only come out at night.
Some think they're always right.
Some are brazen.
Some have hearts as dark as a raven.
Some are free to conceal who they truly are.
Some have gone too far.
Some hide their true face;
Some can just walk away without a trace.
Some will do anything – even cheat – to win a race.

Some have no grace.

Some are free to be themselves,

At any time, at any place.

Some just don't care;

Any compassion from them is rare.

Some just stand there and glare.

Some can't control themselves and let their anger flare.

Some fly high.

Some are sly.

Some mock those who cry.

Some always lie.

Some will try anything for a sweet prize.

Some can't let anyone get ahead,

Let anyone else rise.

Some sink in greed,

Some refuse to fight, to bleed.

Their hungry hearts can never be freed.

Some drown in darkness and debauchery.

Some believe in victory, in treachery.

Some love riches and gold.

Some would walk all over the young and the old.

Some are cowardly. Some are bold.

Some are free to do as they desire.

Some don't care about the innocent's pain and ire.

Some don't ever tire.

Some don't burn with the fire.

Some are only interested in their intent;

Some surpass to a great extent.

Some are born to be liars.

Some grow wings even though they are not meant to be fliers.

Some give no choice.

Some show no poise.

Some have lost themselves to rage.

Some fail at every stage.

Some never grow with age.

Some can be silent;

Some can be violent.

Some are afraid of reality.

Some live in obscurity.

Some have lost all sense of clarity.

Some hide in the shadows.

Some pretend to be mellow.

Some are surrounded in secrets and intrigue.

Some have never tasted fatigue.

Some have too much to keep.

Some are afraid to sleep.

Some choose to dream forever;

Some refuse to wake up – ever.

Some abandon frankness and embrace the fake;

Some will do anything for their sake.

Some take everything and brake;

Some don't believe in sharing or giving;

They just take.

Some are free to wonder.

Some easily plunder.

Some don't care about making a blunder.

Some escape safe and sound;

Some will go round and round.

Some don't believe.

Some just leave.

Some don't stop; they keep going further.

Some think it their right to steal,

To murder.

Some make a hasty run.

It is hard to run from the sun.

Some must pay for what they have done.

Justice is not a game;

It cannot be won.

Everything must come to order;

The strength of the innocent grows bolder.

The horizon becomes broader.

Some begin to falter;

Scenarios begin to alter.

It is then that the light shall be replenished;

All doubts will be banished.

Some are punished.

Some then learn to walk tall,

Walk straight;

They must carry honesty's weight.

Or the righteous shall come along to rid them of their nasty trait.

FREE

Wake up; face the sun!

It's time to let go and have fun.

Open the door! Let your destiny in.

May your tale begin! May you win!

Let your fear spread its wings and take flight.

Listen to the laughter, to the light.

It shall guide you to your dreams, to delight.

Answer the evening with yearning and hope,

For in your dreams you may hang by a longer rope.

Do not lie; it's a slippery slope.

Only truth and courage can help you cope.

WATCH

I watch as the world unravels, as the soul travels.

I watch as humanity begins to bicker and fight.

I watch the battle between the dark and the light.

I watch the clouds cry rain;

I watch as the raindrops fall in vain.

I watch as old, rickety chairs unhinge.

I watch as people carelessly toss them aside.

I cringe.

I watch as the soul shines.

I watch as the heart whines.

I watch people learn to ignore important signs.

This is the era of dependence,

I watch as people give up their independence with a vengeance.

They ask, *Why bother when all our gadgets are there to show the way?*

Why bother having a say?

I watch as continents unite.

I watch as stars dance in the night.

I watch as the innocent begin to bite.

I watch as the birds walk on earth,

As they give up flight.

I watch as brilliance shines bright.

I watch as the line begins to disappear between wrong and right.

I watch as the shadows grow long.

I watch as nature alters its song.

I watch as the weak grow strong.

I watch as the lion begins to accept his cage.

I watch as happiness is destroyed by rage.

Strange how it all ends on the same page!

FASHION

In this world of fashion,

What value does novelty hold?

Fashion can be warm, or cold.

When it comes to fashion, there is a difference

between the modest and the bold.

Fashion can draw a crowd.

Fashion can make one humble,

Make one proud.

Fashion can be aggressive.

Fashion can also be simple and passive.

It comes in different varieties, like a feast.

Fashion can be like a beast:

Cut off one head, and another shall arise.

Fashion loves to rise.

Fashion can make noise;

It can show poise.

Fashion can be silent; it can come without a sound.

Fashion makes a complete round.

Fashion changes from season to season.

To support fashion, one doesn't need a reason.

Inspired by the cultures of this world, fashion can create fusion.

Fashion can cause confusion.

Fashion is easy to mock.

It works around the clock.

Fashion is wrought with attention and passion.

It differs from person to person,

Nation to nation.

Fashion causes elation.

It stirs sensation and lifts the soul;

Fashion plays more than one role.

Fashion is a divided street.

It can be both bitter and sweet.

Fashion battles its way through the cold and the heat.

Fashion can be messy and neat.

It unites us with the daring, the bold.

It separates us from the humble and the modest.

Fashion can hold its ground.

It has all the keys to open doors.

It travels around.

Fashion is surrounded by gossip and scandal.

Fashion is a flame that sits atop a candle.

Fashion can be tricky to handle.

If it were in fashion, one would proudly adorn oneself with dust;

One would support and wear rust.

Fashion is a way to fit in.

It is a way to begin.

Fashion can both lose and win.

The world of fashion is unique;

It has no twin.

Fashion never dies;

It can always come back.

When it comes to comfort, fashion can terribly lack.

It holds no respect for those who slack.

Fashion can require sophistication.

Fashion never takes a vacation.

It can be loose or tight.

It goes away without a fight.

Fashion never stops moving;

It never stops growing.

Fashion is a tool used to rise above the rest.

You want what you wear to define you;

It becomes a test.

Fashion is not always about the best.

Fashion takes no break, no rest.

Fashion can be found in the north, south, east and west.

Fashion needs no invitation;

It quickly builds a nest.

What fashion dictates becomes a statement;

It becomes the norm.

Fashion can wear fur when the weather's warm.

Fashion can sizzle out quickly,

Or it can take the world by storm.

To travel, fashion needs no train, no car.

But can fashion ever go too far?

Forget what is right:

What is wrong?

Even amid silence,

Sing a song!

Some would disagree.

Some would agree.

Call fashion *an ugly tree.*

Its branches crawl over tradition,

Alter and corrupt its richness.

It's a desecration of culture that is hard to witness.

Some call fashion *a beautiful tree,*

A way to move forward and feel free.

A leader from birth, fashion is ahead.

It is not something to dread.

Fashion can be easily followed.

Sometimes it is bought, sometimes borrowed.

If put on heat for too long, fashion begins to burn.

Sometimes new concepts deserve a turn.

For some fashion is meaningless,

Empty and loose.

For some, it's as absolute as a tight knot, and filled with clues.

Fashion could be a façade; to learn the truth,

one must look behind the curtain.

Fashion can be certain.

One thing, though, is true:

Within reason nothing can be a burden;

With boundaries nothing strays too far.

If harmony can be reached,

Take it as a fact: no sensitivities would ever be breached.

NO PROMISES

You will get no promises from me.

I am what I appear to be.

If you wish to fly, I shall honour your wings.

I'll stand by you no matter what the future brings.

With you, my heart sings.

I can make no promises.

I can conquer all contests with your voice in my head.

I'd leave my doubts behind and follow you instead.

With you beside me, why worry about the rest?

Life is no longer a harrowing test.

With you, I'd gladly build a nest.

But don't expect things to be easy, to be the best.

I can promise nothing to you. I live my life on the edge.

If you wish to stand beside me, it would probably be on a ledge.

Nothing will ever come between us.

No rift, no wedge.

I can make no promises to you,

None that I can keep.

You are all I see when I sleep.

If you join me, you'll fall far. You'll fall deep.

I know my words are hollow, that they are steep.

I can make no promises to you.

You have nothing to achieve by standing beside me – nothing to win,

Nothing to gain.

Don't you know your sacrifices would be in vain?

That one day you would be tired of this strain?

With me, it shall always rain.

I can make no promises to you.

Uncertainty follows me like a determined friend.

I always stand out, no matter how hard I try to fit in,

To blend.

With you beside me, the nights are no longer dark. The days are bright.

My spirit wants to leave my flesh behind and take flight.

You make me look forward to each day with renewed hope.

No matter what the day brings, I know I can cope.

I now look forward to each day with yearning.

You make me look forward to the morning.

I believe you have won me over without warning.

I can read you as clearly as a book.

The moment you noticed me, my world shifted on its axis.

It wobbled. It shook.

It happened with a single glance, a single look.

You have no idea what you did, what you took.

I can make no promises to you,

But you're the reason I left behind my old ways,

The old days.

Towards you I drifted.

My criteria, my thoughts shifted.

My spirit soared; it lifted.

Surely you won me over, much like a game.

What can I say?

I shall never be me again. I shall never be the same.

I can make no promises,

But I'd always honour your ambition,

Your contribution.

For, as much as I am hollow, you are someone I'd follow.

I can promise you neither safety nor danger.

You know me. To you I am no stranger.

I can promise you neither the ambiguity of

darkness nor the gleam of sunshine.

I'll always ensure that you're fine.

I can promise you no glitter, no fame.

Everything will change for you;

Nothing would remain the same.

With me, the only certain thing you'll have, you'll know,

That would be my name.

With me, you'll get no picture – just an empty frame.

I have no direction, no aim.

I can make no promises to you.

But with me, you will always be free of guilt and blame.

If I am fire, then you are my flare, my flame.

No matter where this path may lead,

You are whom I want, whom I need.

Our doubts are easy to feed.

As they topple, they don't scar, don't bleed.

I know they won't return once they leave.

I can make no promises to you.

Staying with me comes with a high cost.

Don't tell me all that you have lost.

Before you came, I was empty.

Now I have plenty.

I am the answer to all your questions, the wood to your tree.

With you, I am no longer limited. I am free.

There is so much I'd sacrifice, all for your sake.

There is so much for you to choose from,

So much more to conquer, to take!

But I can make no promises.

There is so much at stake.

Some promises are not easy to make.

I'd rather keep it real than make it fake.

The top of this mountain is narrow and small.

Don't come up here; please, do not fall.

I can make no promises to you.

I have nothing much to offer, to give.

All I ask of you is to *live*.

I am harsh and stiff,

But I'd never hurt you over a silly tiff.

In order to stay together, we must stand united on the edge of this cliff.

I can make no promises.

The first time I saw you, your eyes glimmered in the sun.

It was then I knew there was nowhere to run.

I knew I had found my balance, my light.

There was no doubt in my mind. I'd never let go of you without a fight.

I thought I was dreaming when I first saw you sitting by the lake.

I didn't want the dream to be over. I didn't want to wake.

I can't promise anything to you.

You'll have to take a chance to stand by my side,

But I shall stand aside and give you room,

Be it high or low, narrow or wide.

Here, you can grow. You can hide.

If it doesn't work out, don't say I lied.

Let it go. Just let it slide.

You are welcome to this whenever you please.

This is not something that can be moved by the wind or the breeze.

I will arrange this room for you,

Much like an ocean makes room for its elusive tide.

I'd do it with pleasure – not something that I have to tolerate or abide.

I cannot promise to be your light in the dark,

But I shall help you reach your mark.

With me, you will not gain power,

Yet you'll sit high on my tower.

There will be no promises of strength.

I cannot give you a fixed time, a fixed length.

I cannot say how long we shall stay together.

This journey is difficult to measure.

It will need precision; it is not something to be done at leisure.

I cannot promise you a thing. Yet to me, you are everything.

You are my treasure.

Your spirit beckons me to accept all the things I wish to embrace.

No matter where I look, I can clearly hear your voice and see your face.

To me you are as strong as a tree.

Your eyes are as deep as the sea.

If you wish to unlock me, I shall gladly hand over that precious key.

Only you can set me free!

I can promise you nothing,

Not even a plea if you wish to go, to leave.

I don't wear my emotions on my face or on my sleeve.

In order to keep this up, you will have to let go and believe.

It is too early yet to grieve.

I was afraid to lose you the first time I closed my eyes and slept.

When I saw you again, my spirit breathed a sigh of relief. It wept.

I cannot stand to watch you cry.

I'd always want your cheeks to remain dry.

When I see your tears,

I am faced with one of my worst fears.

When I see your smile,

Everything becomes possible; there is no more room for denial.

I cannot promise you anything,

Not even joviality or fun.

You make me walk, make me run.

I am yours. I am done.

I shall shoulder all your burdens;

May they weigh a kilo or a ton.

The moment you laid your eyes on me I was yours. I was won.

Even in winter, I can feel myself burn.

I cannot promise you anything,

But your affection is something I'd work my hardest to earn.

Loving you is new to me, but it is not difficult to learn.

My eyes follow you everywhere you go.

For you, I am prepared for all, be it high or low.

Your gaze keeps me rooted to the ground even when the

earth starts to tremble, when the wind begins to blow.

With you next to me things begin to fall in line. They begin to flow.

I no longer wish to take it slow.

I know I shall remain. I shall not fade.

I am not afraid.

It is all because of your devotion, your aid.

I can make no promises to you.

None at all.

Yet you have made me cross all my limits. Even ones I didn't know I had.

You taught me to see the good in everything, not just the bad.

I would always strive to see you happy, never sad.

Mysteries begin to make sense when you are here.

Losing you is something I dread...I fear.

Whenever I need you, you're always near.

With you next to me, everything becomes logical and clear.

I can make no promises to you,

But to you I am an open door.

I will always answer your calls.

I'll be your home without walls.

I can make no promises to you,

But you make me feel light as a feather.

Like the leaves of autumn, like the flakes of snow,

We shall fall together.

If you leave, then I will follow you.

I won't ask you to stay.

The transition will be simple.

I will not ask you to walk into a fray.

Your heart can't keep me away.

Without you I am afraid I'd lose my way.

You are my night. You are my day.

For you, I am easy to slay.

I can make no promises, none at all.

Being with me would be a huge change. A difficult task!

I do not have much to give but I have little to ask.

I am not easy to break. I am hard as stone.

All this time, I've been alone.

You live in my flesh, my soul and my bone.

You can call me your own.

I can make no promises to you.

By now you know my stance.

This is real, not just some meaningless dance.

I found my home in you at first glance.

I wish for you to stay, yet for you to move on.

I want you beside me, yet I want you gone.

You know you are entitled to more.

You have a spirit that deserves to soar.

A life that is fuller, that is better.

A sea that is deeper, that is wetter.

I cannot promise anything to you.

Not even glee or hope.

I am but a slippery slope.

As much as my words may hurt or may sting,

I don't want to hide anything from you, not a single thing.

Who knows what the future will bring?

We must take one another's hand. We must take a stand.

Who knows where this shall take us,

Or where we shall land?

In silence, I yearn to hear your voice.

When I am clumsy, I look forward to your elegance, your poise.

I cannot promise anything to you.

I do not know if I will ever change.

But for you I'd expand my capabilities, my range.

When it becomes dark, you are someone I seek.

With you, things become less maudlin and less bleak.

Your ire breaks my fences.

It leaves me open for attack.

You handle my vulnerability with great tact.

You are not a figment of my imagination. You are fact.

I can make no promises to you,

For I am water and you are oil.

Put together, we ignite. Things begin to boil.

Our bond is strong. It is not something someone can foil.

I cannot promise you anything.

Yet I'd shower you with wealth and affection.

My soul shall always find you. It needs no direction.

If I had a heart, you would have made it forget to beat.

It is your turn to take its place;

It is your turn to accept this seat.

Tell me: was conquering me an easy feat?

KEEP LOOKING FOR WINTER

They say warmth kindles the heart, the soul;

It makes one feel whole.

But what if sparks lead to fire?

It can lead to consequences both lasting and dire.

If you're looking for winter, keep going higher.

The heat of summer quickly makes room in our hearts.

The heat is sorely missed when the winter starts.

The heat penetrates all that was once frigid and bold.

It shows no mercy to things that are cold.

It is difficult to escape once the summer begins to take hold.

Winter continues to fight for its survival. It does not give in, does not fold.

Heat melts away all that you are.

Cold protects you; it returns you to your former glory.

It leads to a better story.

Strong and sharp, ice keeps its foes away.

It keeps them at bay.

In the absence of heat, ice can remain as long as it wishes to stay.

But beware!

Unlike heat, ice is easy to defeat, to slay.

Nothing is as vulnerable to heat, as is ice.

Just as nothing is more vulnerable to the truth, as are lies.

The snow blankets all that hurts, all that ails.

Winter remains pure. It never fails.

Keep searching.

The cold shall take over once your glory, your winter is found.

Just like summer, winter comes without fuss, without sound.

Soon the snow begins to spread. It is all around.

Heat destroys ice, leaving behind nothing

but pavements that look stained.

It looks like it rained.

When the ice stands in its glory, it is the victor.

Keep looking for winter.

SYMPHONY OF
A WARRIOR'S HEART

If you want peace, then you must be willing to fight.

If you want love and joy, you must look towards the light.

When the night begins, it must be faced with honesty and courage.

There is no room for fear and rage.

In life one must be prepared for all,

At any time, at any stage.

If you despise hate, don't hold back your love until it's too late.

If your actions can help save the world,

You must be prepared to carry their weight.

In the end, there is no escaping fate.

STOP

I cannot stop.

My doubts are still ruling, sitting on top.

I know I have moved far and beyond all that

was once alright, once allowed.

I don't understand how I allowed my judgment to cloud.

I am neither satisfied nor proud.

Have I gone too far to come back?

Surrounded by my mistakes, my shadows,

Is everything now black?

In my absence, who was there to pick up the slack?

To leave behind the burning desire,

Or to leave behind all that lights me on fire?

Are those my only choices?

It's a good thing then that my disappointments don't have voices.

They would've whined.

Cast their shadows on all that could've once shined.

Have I not paid enough?

I believe I have been properly punished, properly fined.

How could I have been so blind?

Things which are most important to us are never hard to find.

I know all this; yet I cannot just stop.

I have come too far and too high.

Whatever I have done, I cannot deny.

This hasn't been a treat.

I wish I could hasten my retreat.

The moments of clarity are becoming shorter and rare.

This emptiness is becoming easier to bear.

Am I beyond all sympathy and all care?

Have I shed away all that I was, all that was good?

Am I now stripped bare?

This trip has been an ugly fare.

Yet still I cannot stop.

More dust is needed to destroy this particular crop.

Perhaps ...

Perhaps I am not ready to admit it has been a flop.

I left behind gold in search for silver;

To get there, I crossed every road, every river.

Reminded by this, I shiver.

If I could go back, I would sacrifice more to be given a second chance,

Or at the very least a second glance.

It is this thought that gives me pause.

In order to stop, I have finally found my cause.

Slowly, I gradually descend.

It will take time to find myself.

I have tried too long to blend.

My principles, once strong and tall, I forced them to bend.

I am now awake. I shall destroy this trend.

I am halfway away from disaster, halfway back to my past.

I believe once I get there, my happiness will finally last.

WINGS

It was too long ago when I first spread my wings and flew,

The days were endless and nights were few.

The sinners faced doom, and the innocents ruled as much as they could.

I could just spread my wings and fly, no matter what mood.

Now my flights end too soon.

It was too long ago that I flew to the moon.

A new era dawned, and all my paradise turned to ruins.

The rays of light became so delicate and rare.

It's been so long since my wings tasted air.

However, as the sun shines in my long silken hair,

My wings spread wider.

No matter the despair, I will always be a fighter,

Even if I'm the only flier.

My laughter echoes in the surrounding air.

My eyes turn brighter as my wings take me up,

Take me higher.

They say the road to hell is paved with good intentions ...
Then where does the righteous human stand?

THE ROAD TO HEAVEN

Life is temporary; heaven is forever.

Good deeds are the way to go.

Learn to say something other than *no*.

Care for those who deserve it.

For those who don't deserve it – care for them too.

After all is said and done, only your heart remains true.

How much does the heart weigh when filled with good, virtuous deeds?

It is something every soul needs.

However, good deeds are not burdensome.

They make you feel light.

They make you feel right.

When it gets dark, they shine bright.

They set you free.

The road to heaven is paved with freedom.

Wrongdoings lead to culpability, which in turn darkens the heart.
They should say the road to hell is paved with guilt.

STILL

In this dazzling world of fire and heat,
So cold some seasons can get.
It is difficult to tell time when the days and nights have met.
Humanity stands in silence on grounds rickety and wet.
The changes are keenly felt when the ice begins to melt.
It's strange how winds still bring forth swirls and howls!
Birds still fly during the day – and at night, owls.

DON'T GO

Don't go.

Darkness lies ahead in wait.

Don't take the bait.

The battle here remains strong.

I need you in case something goes wrong.

This battle is taking too long.

It rages on; it is everywhere.

Stopping it is not something someone would dare.

All rules are broken; nothing seems fair.

Rather than settling, the dust is everywhere. It is in the air.

The darkness pushes on, obstinate and resilient.

The light pushes back, strong and valiant.

Don't go.

The journey is uncertain ahead.

Won't you stay here instead?

Up ahead, it would be too dark for you to see.

Don't go. Stay with me.

We need you here.

This battle will only get more severe.

The smoke may take some time to clear.

Don't go. Stay with me. Stay near.

We are not without hope, without fear.

This battle has taken so much already.

How are you still so calm, so steady?

You are always attentive, always ready.

Someday this battle will end, and then you'll move on.

You'll be gone.

The dark forces ahead should dread your arrival.

For the light, you would be their hope, their survival.

I want you here; I want you there.

I know you'll do the right thing, that you care.

I want you to fight, yet stay behind.

The battle will rage between my heart and my mind.

Don't go. Not without me.

The battlefield is the only place for us to be.

We are the fish in this sea.

Don't go alone.

Trust me.

You don't have to carry this burden on your own.

You don't have to fight alone.

PAST, PRESENT, AND FUTURE

If you long to repeat old history,

You must have it in your heart to give up on life's mystery.

To dance to the sweet melodies of the past,

One must abandon unseen, but perhaps meaningful moments,

That in the future could last.

The present is nothing but an unfelt test,

All about choices

Of what would be best.

The uncertain future becomes difficult to sample, to taste,

Where everything from the past is laid to waste.

BULB

I am light; I am bright.

I work night and day;

I help show the way.

I am forever delicate, forever fragile;

You'd be disappointed if you expect me to be agile.

I can be narrow; I can be wide.

I am round everywhere; I have no side,

My abode is made of glass. I have nothing to hide.

When you shake me, I rattle from someplace deep;

I never sleep.

I can fit left or right,

Made to move up or down.

I can be found anywhere,

City or town.

Blinded by my own light, I see nothing when I look down.

I never smile, never frown.

I must answer when my services are in need.

I eat little; I am easy to feed.

When I break, I don't bleed.

I am a welcome guest;

With me around, the light can rest.

How I am used, it is not up to me to choose.

I have little to gain, little to lose.

I have no mind, so how can I judge?

Once I am fixed, I cannot budge.

I cannot identify what is right, what is wrong.

I do not have a voice. I cannot sing a song.

My shadow is sometimes short, sometimes long.

No matter where I go,

I shall always have a spot waiting for me; I shall always belong.

I am known to be weak, to be strong.

I come in many colours;

I am not limited to just white and yellow.

I can be dazzling or mellow.

I have no depth. I am shallow.

I am unwelcome where secrets are stored.

I do not know what it means to be excited or bored.

I shed light on justice and crime;

I am blind to day, to time.

I burn from within so I can bring forth light.

When the internal battle is over,

It ends without warning, without a fight.

Who knows where I'll be tomorrow?

My absence can sometimes remind of bitter memories and old sorrow.

Wherever there is dark, I must follow.

When it comes to my space, I do not share;

One must handle me with care.

Decisions are best made in my presence, when I am around.

I work without a sound.

I defeat the dark for it can invoke fear, betray our eyes.

The shadows play host to lies.

If I fall, then I shall shatter;

When handled with care, I work better.

Don't break me,

Keep me safe and whole;

Only then can I complete my role.

I have just one weakness, one enemy;

Listen closely, for I don't have many:

If there is one thing I cannot abide, then that is water.

It throws my world into turmoil.

We don't mix, much like water and oil.

If my system is compromised by water,

I can no longer maintain discipline and order.

I don't disappoint when all my requirements and needs are met;

Don't get me wet.

My light is free; it cannot be trapped in a net.

When it comes to battling the dark,

I am your best bet!

HAPPINESS

Happiness is brief; it is fleeting.

If life is a heart, happiness keeps it beating.

In a world so fraught with hardships, happiness brings peace.

It locks all doors to melancholy and gloom. It holds all keys.

Happiness puts the soul at ease.

Happiness is easy to please.

When the heart is heavy, happiness lifts the burden away.

Sadness is a wicked beast,

One that only happiness can slay.

Humans are built of clay,

So what is happiness built of?

It is so strong that it can knock down any door.

It can make your heart soar;

It can make it roar.

Because it's so fleeting, happiness holds a special place in the heart.

It is more precious than any priceless art.

Happiness is a moody, temporary guest; it doesn't stay for long.

To keep it in our lives, happiness must be made to feel like it can belong.

For this, the soul needs to be strong.

Sadness is undesirable and unwelcome,

Out of sight but always there.

Happiness, on the other hand, should be handled with care:

It is so easy to drive it away.

Happiness takes offence at the slightest wrong sway.

Happiness helps show the way.

Happiness is welcome night and day.

In order to greet it more often, you must keep

all doors to your heart wide open.

You must cherish happiness like a fragile glass,

But even then it doesn't always last.

Sometimes, happiness can make it easier for you to bear your past.

Happiness is deep and vast.

Happiness takes its time; it is never slow, never fast.

Happiness can come in many a layer.

Beware!

Pride and arrogance can get in the way of obtaining this elusive treasure.

It would be an opportunity lost for boundless pleasure.

Happiness works hard.

It never takes time off for leisure.

Pressure to obtain it is the same as driving it away.

Any attempt to run towards it would drive the two of you farther apart.

Happiness is fleeting;

Achieving it is no easy part.

When your soul dances to the music of life,

It is happiness that is pulling the strings of your heart.

It is what adds the sugar to your tart.

GAME

What makes one a loser?

A frown on the forehead, or a bitter grin?

A smile on the face, despite the fact they didn't win?

What about the winner?

How are they defined?

For one, they are refined.

They don't have to be polite or kind,

But they must have a talented mind.

Before a game can begin,

One must win from within.

So which is more important?

A smile on the face,

Or victory at the end of the race?

A trophy in hand?

After flying for so long, it must feel good to land.

In a game, so much can go wrong.

A game can be short or long.

It can be weak or strong.

If game is a song, then its player is the singer.

They could leave behind their mark or linger.

Games can alter with just a move of a finger.

Game is like a tunnel:

No one knows what lies in wait,

Triumph or defeat?

Victory offers only one seat.

Odds are something every player should beat.

When it comes to a game, things are rarely neat.

We play games, but in the end, the game begins to play back;

It shows no mercy to those who slack.

A player can turn the game around;

A game can threaten all that is safe and sound.

No player admires defeat.

To win, some players even cheat.

It is wrong to do so,

To do anything to strike down any obstacle, any wall.

Some players don't care for the game;

They just want to remain true,

Stand tall.

On the seat of victory, only one can sit.

In order to win,

All players must remain fit.

They have to control their wit.

To win, the intent needs to be clear.

One cannot play host to doubt or fear.

Victory is something that all players seek.

Victory is something only the winner can keep.

On the surface the game is merely material;

Underneath, it becomes real.

When players meet, like lightning, they cause a dazzling flash;

It is something to watch when souls clash.

When rules begin to bend,

The integrity of the game has met its end.

The game remains the same even as players change.

Each player brings with them a new range.

Games continue even as players tire,

When it comes to a game, don't play with the rules;

Don't play with fire.

Every game has two kinds of victory, two kinds of defeat:

One for the world and one for the soul.

A game plays more than one role.

LOST

I wander through the woods considering your words.

My soul took years to fly up in the sky alongside those wonderful birds.

Your voice brings warmth to my core;

Your words confuse me to the bone.

I feel so lost,

So soft to the touch.

Inside, I hurt so very much.

I feel so lost.

You promised me happiness,

But in your wake, you leave me in deep sadness.

I feel so lost.

I stood beside you for so long, my eyes wide shut.

For too long,

I found myself in your lies.

I put myself together, all the broken pieces.

I won't let you break me apart.

Love should never have been this hard.

Hot all over, frozen inside.

It's all out in the open. I have nothing to hide.

You were my beacon of light.

I lost myself because you were my guide.

Finding my way back was easier said than done.

But I would brave it, rather than run.

SECURITY

There is such security in your lies.

Things begin to look bleak when despair flies.

You know just what to say.

Your words turn black into white,

Night into day.

Empty words hold such sway,

They force hope to remain, to stay.

Such security is false.

It refuses to answer when hope calls.

When doubts and disappointments begin to blend,

Such security means nothing in the end.

It lacks soul, lacks purity.

In the end, hope is the best security.

TREASURE

I sail across the sea of fortune and treasure;
I do it with pleasure.
I watch the golden hue above me as the sun begins to set.
I shall have a great time, I bet.
The sapphire sky continues to shine as I smile.
I continue onwards, inch by inch,
Mile by mile.
The jade green ocean can hear echoes of my laughter as I continue to sail.
It is a simple task. I do not wish to fail.
The silvery clouds twinkle delightfully overhead, as I make way to shore.
I sailed and sailed but didn't find the riches that I was promised.
Was I chasing false lore?

MY SPACE

In my space filled with laughter and joy,
I'm no-one's puppet, no-one's toy.
The wrong remains wrong, and the right remains right.
All I need is within my grasp, my sight.
The loose remains loose too, and tight remains tight.
Everything is perfectly balanced and fair;
Everything is simple yet detailed, layer by layer.
In my space nothing is too hard to bear.
I protect my space fiercely. Breaching it isn't
something someone would dare.
Treat it with care.
In my space, all necessities of life are easily available.
There is no doubt, no trouble,
There is no waste, no rubble.
Everything is perfect.
I could forever live in my very own bubble.

DEAR MOTHER

I dedicate this poem to my mother

My dear mother,

Since the moment we were born, you have always been there.

You are kind. You are fair.

You are a gift for all. You make us stand tall.

With your guidance, we can overcome any obstacle, any wall.

You pull us back from the edge; you don't let us fall.

We'd always answer your call.

You are our ship in a wide ocean;

You are known for your boundless love and devotion.

You have always been there for us whenever we needed you the most;

With you, we can never be lost.

Your love is open and free; it has no limit, no cost.

My dear mother,

Your warmth soothes our soul,

Changes our world and makes us strong.

To us you are perfect; you can do no wrong.

My dear mother,

You worry for us when all is well.

What is best for us, only you can tell.

With a few encouraging words from you, we

can travel lands and conquer seas.

Only you can reach us, unlock us;

Only you can hold all the keys.

My dear mother,

With you beside us,

The rain falls lightly; it falls down straight.

The mountains are no longer heavy; they lose their weight.

The sun shines daily. It shines bright.

When it gets dark, you become our guide, our light.

You keep our fears at bay when it is dark, when it is night.

You are worth every fight!

My dear mother,

The moon loses its radiance; it forgets to glow when you are not around.

There isn't enough warmth, enough light to be found.

You strengthen ties,

Give us hope when the heart cries.

You know the difference between our truths, our lies.

Without you there is no joy, no meaning to our life;

Our world is lost to disharmony and strife.

My dear mother,

When our problems arise, you come forth with the best solutions.

You save us from our illusions.

You are valuable in ways that cannot be explained,

Cannot be defined.

Your love and your sincerity make us honest,

Make us refined.

When we call for you, you are easy to find.

You are forever compassionate, forever kind.

Only you can understand what lies in our hearts,

In our minds.

With your love, all conflicts are won;

You are brighter than the sun.

You taught us to walk, to run.

You introduced us to laughter, to fun.

For us, you always want the best.

With you, we can be who we are.

Life is not a test.

With you beside us, our dilemmas become few.

Everything seems fresh and new.

No matter how obstinate we may get, only you can get through to us;

Only you can change our view.

You are the first thing we hear, the first thing we see.

You are our desert, our sea.

You taught us colours, the difference between black and white.

You taught us to take our first bite.

Your gentle attention and devotion change our reality,

You give our minds clarity.

You reshape our perspective.

You are forever generous in your love; you never discriminate.

You are never selective.

You lift our hearts, elevate our souls,

You help with our achievements, our goals.

You can do anything; play any role.

You taught us how to learn;

You are the tree to our fern.

You are the music to our song.

When you are with us, no calamity,

No disaster can last long.

No matter how much we lose our way,

We shall always find ourselves in you.

We shall always belong.

My dear mother,

With you next to us, nothing is too high or too low.

Nothing is too fast or too slow.

You anchor us when the wind starts to blow.

You are our light and our glow.

You never push us, never pull us back.

You complete us in all the things that we lack.

Your love keeps us in our best form.

You are our shelter in a storm.

No matter what we may have done, you never turn us away.

You love us anyway.

Your love is absolute;

It is not something anyone can pollute.

Your love for us remains the same every season.

You show us logic. You show us reason.

You keep us away from all that can cause tension.

From you, there is no need to hide.

There is no lie, no pretention.

When we fall, it is you waiting to catch us at the bottom.

You carry us in your embrace like the wind

carries the fallen leaves of autumn.

To you our soul is bare.

You handle it with such delicate care.

Our lives would be torn asunder if you weren't keeping it together.

We have achieved so much in life because we stayed true, together.

My dear mother,

Within us, you are a cause of elation.

Your loyalty shall never move, never budge,

Your love will never doubt, never judge.

You are the sand in the desert, the water in a rough, dry wasteland.

We take our first steps holding your hand.

No matter what façade we put up, you can always see behind the curtain.

Your love and support are certain.

Whatever life throws at us, you must not take blame;

Our mistakes are ours to claim.

Your love is impossible to measure. Who can count grains of sugar, of salt?

You are without fault.

With strength derived from you, we can overcome any challenge,

Any height.

You are always a magnificent sight.

We cannot fall apart with you holding us together;

All our troubles and burdens vanish.

We become light as a leaf, as a feather.

You prepare us for every scenario, every weather.

The world may change,

But one thing shall never alter:

A mother's love shall never falter.

You are a piece of art carved by nature's best hand.

You always fly, never land.

You give hope when the night chases the daylight away.

You are your own person; you follow no one's

sway. You help us find our way.

We obey you in a second, on a single say.

Despite all that we have seen and felt, you make our day.

When we were younger, you taught us how to smile, how to play.

You gave us our first toy.

You give such joy.

You are someone we can always depend on,

Always trust.

You bring out the best in us when we are at our worst.

My dear mother,

You are intelligent in ways that cannot be defined.

You have a gentle soul, a strong mind.

You can make our qualms; our fears disappear.

With your help, our fragile courage begins to form; it begins to appear.

You stop us from going too far.

In our world, you shine like a star.

You are patient when we complain, when we whine.

You can make all our worries fall in line.

You right our wrongs. Make it alright, make it fine.

You see us without trying.

In your eyes, we are always youthful, always flying.

With you there is only truth – no lying.

Your love cannot be bought.

It is something that only comes naturally;

It cannot be taught.

You can make us climb a tower, a mountain.

Swim in a wide ocean, a simple fountain.

Life under your guidance becomes simple and straight.

Your love is always on time;

It is never delayed, never late.

You only teach us joy and love, never anger, never hate.

You find depth even in a pond.

Nothing can shake our bond.

You know how to pull us back when we create a fuss;

Your words bring joy to us.

All those times when we were difficult, when we made it hurt,

You were always kind, never curt.

All those times we disappointed you,

You never let it show.

In the middle of July

You can make it snow.

My dear mother,

You vanquish our doubts, give us relief;

Our bouts of hysteria remain brief.

You guide us when things begin to fall apart.

You have always told us to follow our hearts.

You turn our faces away when the sun is too bright.

You teach us to do our best,

To do what is right.

Your love remains strong even when everything else begins to drift;

You can repair any rift.

You sooth our doubts and fears,

Wipe away our sweat and tears.

You laugh when we laugh; you cry when we cry.

You can make us run or make us fly.

You can always tell when we lie.

Your love can defeat our enemies, send them away.

For us, you keep them at bay.

You are the reason we hang on.

Or else we'd be swept away; we'd be gone.

My dear mother,

You respect what we choose.

You are always there when we win and when we lose.

You help us figure out all the clues.

When our world's upside down,

You set us back on track without a frown.

You taught us to laugh when we saw our first clown.

My dear mother,

A single hug from you can lock away any trouble.

You save us from the rubble.

You are who keeps us stable.

You see us without bias, without label.

My dear mother,

We always have a home in your heart.

Your touch can take away our burn;

We need you at every turn.

Your love is incomparable.

No one can touch your calibre.

You are the reason we walk straight,

The reason we do great.

No matter how strong the winds or the current may become,

We can always sail.

You take away our fear, we are no longer afraid to fail.

My dear mother,

No words are enough when it comes to describing you.

You are thoughtful. You are soulful.

When we fall sick, you nurse us back to health.

Forget about the riches of the world,

You are our wealth.

My dear mother,

Your love is forever there.

You always care.

Your love, like the sun, burns bright;

Like the moon, it glows white.

My dear mother,

You always bring a smile to our faces.

With you next to us, we can win any race.

You teach us poise and grace.

You will love, protect and guide us till the end of our days.

You are there for us.

Always.

DREAMS

My dreams are not my own.
They are yesterday's,
When joyous were the days,
When the world wanted me to rise,
To fly.
It was lovely; I couldn't deny.
Then, the stars fell from the sky, and I was one of them.
My place was taken by those who envied me,
More stars in the endless sky.
I am no longer up so high.
Oh, how I wish it were all a lie.

PLAN

How can I plan this thing called life
When nothing ever goes according to plan?
It feels like I've been flying forever,
Searching for a place to land.
Sometimes I feel like I've been climbing ceaselessly,
And I have yet to reach the top.
No matter what,
I keep trying. I never stop.
How can I plan my future,
When any control over my present remains elusive?
Theories are all well and good,
But nothing ever seems conclusive.
What seems too far away is sometimes closer than you might think.
Sometimes life leaves you standing at the brink.
Life is an experiment,
One that is hard to control.
Life is a park,
Where we all must stroll.
Life is a test no one is ever prepared for.
Life is an elaborate scheme of circumstances with plenty to go around.
Life is a circle where everything makes a complete round.
So how can I plan a life that cannot be planned?
Simple: I enjoy what I get.

It is the unknown that gives meaning to life,

Much like sharp teeth give edge to a knife.

Life cannot be planned,

So choose a clear surface upon which to land.

Why worry about that which cannot be done?

Why not stay instead of run?

So that's the new plan:

To go with the flow;

Take it slow.

Forget about the plan!

Embrace life and all that it brings forth.

The compass doesn't always point north.

But head on straight and keep the journey smooth.

Plenty of obstacles lie ahead,

So forget about the plan and keep a clear head.

REGRETS

Regrets come silently, yet set our world ablaze.

It is temporary. It is just a phase.

Never say goodbye.

There is no need to sigh.

Face your regrets with a smile.

You will then go a mile.

It may seem hopeless with a burden so heavy.

But never forget: you're just one of many.

The weight shall lift someday; it's just a distance away.

Know this: there is always a way.

Bring on the smile, start at least a mile a day.

TIME

Time cannot be won,

From time, no one can run.

It is with the moon, with the sun.

Time is honest. Time is brutal.

For all, time is fatal.

Time knows no wrong, no right.

Time looks up from below, looks down from a great height.

Time flies away from us, much like a broken kite.

Sometimes time begins to bite.

Time is victorious in every fight.

Time presents an inescapable plight.

Sands of time wash away every failure, every glory.

They introduce a new story.

Time is never sorry.

Time brings forth promises of hope and satisfaction.

Time pays no heed to delays, to distraction.

When the tide of time rises again,

There is something to lose, something to gain.

Time never changes in vain.

Time washes away all that once stood tall.

Time can conquer any wall.

It answers to no call.

Time invites life in.

Time is not something someone can conquer, can win.

Time gives us a chance to end, to begin.

Time knows no love, no hate.

Time is never late.

Time is tied with fate.

Once the curtain lifts, time is difficult to ignore.

Time has plenty in store.

The future is unknown, uncertain,

But one thing is sure:

Every ocean has a shore.

FREE FALL

Fall when you're afraid.

Fall when you're tired.

Fall you must, so you can rise again.

Fall when you believe.

Fall when there's no cure, no relief.

Fall when there's pain.

Fall where there's nothing to gain.

Fall in vain.

Fall when disaster has struck.

Fall when you are out of luck.

Fall you must, so you can rise again.

Fall when it rains.

Fall when the winds are strong.

Fall when you know you are wrong.

Fall for the music, the song.

Fall when you belong.

Fall when you have a lot.

Fall when there is plenty to enjoy.

Fall in utter joy.

Fall when the night has fallen.

Fall when the moon is stolen.

Fall when it is dark.

Fall for the lark!

Fall for a sun too bright.

Fall for the day.

Fall for the night.

Fall for everything that is right.

Fall when the seasons are wet.

Fall when everything is set.

Fall into the net.

Fall for when the dawn and the dusk have met.

Fall for a choice.

Fall for the noise,

Fall for the poise.

Fall for a life that is meaningful and priceless.

Fall when opportunities are lost.

Fall for the cost.

Fall when you have lost the fight.

Fall for a blight.

Fall for the falling star.

Fall far.

Fall you must, so you can rise again.

Fall for it again and again.

Fall for the swindle;

Fall for the trick.

Fall for your pick.

Fall for a tasteless lick.

Fall until you tick.

Fall into a laze.

Fall into a senseless haze.

Fall for the inescapable maze.

Fall for everything that gives you a lift.

Fall for the rift.

Fall for impending victory.

Fall in final defeat.

Fall for sweet pleasure.

Fall for leisure.

Fall for the treasure.

Fall for looming closure.

Fall for a plausible pretend.

Fall, irrevocably, for thine end.

PART

We all have to play out our part, even those we don't understand.

When it comes to some parts, we have to make a stand.

Some parts make us fly; some keep us on land,

Make us walk through fire; walk through sand.

Some parts call for good behaviour;

Some parts mould us into a saviour.

Some parts require courage;

Some parts want us to act our age.

Some parts are easy to play;

Some are difficult to slay.

Some parts make us swim;

Some parts change on a whim.

Some parts are hard to win, to lose;

There are some parts that we don't choose.

There are parts where we must show compassion and care.

Some parts are both easy and hard to bear.

Some parts can make us stronger;

There are some parts that can linger longer.

Some parts are as bright as the sun;

Some parts are hard to handle, to run.

Some parts are light.

Some weigh a ton.

Some parts are serious, some parts are fun.

Some parts are fragrant like fresh berries;

Some parts remind of spices.

Some parts battle vices.

Some parts demand little; others more.

Some parts come with a window or a door.

There are some parts that leave us behind; some that take us far.

Some parts can bathe one in darkness,

Or make them shine like a star.

Every part comes with a choice.

The right and wrong, both demand a voice.

The part that serves best is one closest to your soul, your heart.

That is your path. That is your part.

NOT EVERY QUESTION

When your soul is lost, where does it go?

Is the fall swift or is it slow?

When you are far from your goal, how long before you get there?

Does the wait ever get easier to bear?

When the heart stops beating,

Does a person truly die?

In a world wrought with manipulation,

Can the truth ever sound like a lie?

If a material good is expensive, does it automatically mean that it is better?

For the rich, does it even matter?

What to do when surprises appear at every turn?

When ice touches flesh, why does it burn?

Why are some things so difficult to learn?

When questions take over the mind,

When answers are difficult to find,

Where does one begin to look?

Questions can be long, can be complicated,

Answers can be manipulated, can be fabricated.

But ask away!

Just know this:

Not every question is easy to answer.

SWEETS AND CANDIES

So soft, so delicate,

Hard to duplicate.

Supple and unique, so full of taste,

Preparing it is no matter of haste.

Chocolates, marshmallows,

What is the difference?

Taste and taste, heaven and heaven!

Smooth and crunchy,

All combined in one.

How about a ton?

Too much is too little; too little is painful.

One taste is not enough, merely a prelude to many more:

One for now, some for later, many more in the store.

Sweets are plentiful; one for every occasion.

To munch on one, no one needs a reason.

Every drop is a new sensation.

No boundaries, no blocks, they are found in every nation.

How sweet is that?

WHERE?

Where is the sky when the night is dark?
Where is the sun when the day is bright?
Where to turn to when things fall apart?
Where is sugar in a tart?
Where is the bottom when the fall is slow and long?
Where is music in a song?
Where to go when something is wrong?
Where is the rain when the clouds are murky and dark?
Where is silence in a crowd?
Where is modesty in someone proud?
Where is the light in a long, hollow tunnel?
Where is wind in the summer?
Where is the company in isolation?
Where is victory in desolation?
Where is depth in a pond?
Where is grass on a road?
Where is hope when things get tough?
Where to go when life becomes rough?
Things you can't see, touch, taste, feel –
Where do they go?

STAGE

I slipped off the stage feeling as though I were made of clay.

I didn't know life would be so hard to play.

My legs shook; my heart thudded dully in my chest.

I hoped I'd be okay after a day's rest.

The next morning I woke to find myself feeling queasy.

Did I really think it would be so easy?

But a new day had dawned. The stage once again called my name.

It was time to let go and play my part,

One that was a mixture of sweet sugar and bitter tart.

If I have difficulties, don't blame me. It is not always my fault.

The stage waits for no one. It never grinds to a halt.

Welcome to the play named *Life*,

Where we all stand together, yet we are apart.

It is where I play the role of a soul governed by her conscience,

Her heart.

FEAR

Fear is weak, yet it controls and rules.

When faced with fear, many forget their own tools:

Courage, love, compassion and reasoning.

Fear is a bitter dish that needs a bit of seasoning.

So many mistake them to be fools' tools.

Let them be fools, for their path is straight and right;

For them it's light.

For this light, they are willing to fight.

Easy is the way of the cowardly.

It is dark.

It is night.

Fear has no form;

It should never become the norm.

Fear can be calm or it can create a storm.

So when the shadows call, the weak run in fear.

It's hard for those who actually seem to care.

Their intent is plain and clear.

The night, the dark become difficult to bear.

For the strong, they are afraid of fear.

Courage is a paper; one that keeps away from the scissors of fear.

For the scissor can cut through many things:

Things that are strange and things that are held dear.

Fear is an enemy;

Don't let it in.

Fear can weaken you from within;

Don't let it win.

Fear can be defeated with bravery and strength.

When it comes to fear; it is difficult to measure its length.

Fear should never be invited.

One must brace oneself once fear has been sighted.

Ignoring it doesn't make it go away.

Only trust your courage to show you the way.

BEAUTY

Beauty is subjective.

For some, it's the main objective.

When you look twice in one direction, it's beauty that calls to you.

Beauty is magnetic.

Beauty is enigmatic.

Beauty is dynamic.

Beauty is destructive.

Beauty is constructive.

Beauty is calamity.

Beauty is structure.

Beauty is cold.

Beauty is warm.

Beauty is cozy.

Beauty is home.

Beauty is foreign.

Beauty is civilization.

Beauty is conversation.

Beauty is silence.

Beauty is noise.

Beauty is elegance.

Beauty is poise.

A BUSINESS WORLD

A fetish for wealth and success,

Less for idealists, more for rebels.

It is knowledge that they listen to, for no one spares an ear for a guess.

It is where authority rules, and the rest is a mess.

Houses and offices are polar opposites of each other.

They can no longer exist together.

Whereas animals were once hunted, money is the new prey.

It is all business at the end of the day.

Welcome to a world where business is the new way.

POISON

You are my poison.

I mistook you for my cure.

You were so certain, so sure.

You touched my soul, changed my core.

My heartbeat became faster. I thought it was the right thing.

I had no clue of the pain, the misery you'd bring.

I gave you everything.

This poison is in my blood, on my skin.

I won't let it get far. I won't let it win.

Let the battle begin.

You say you know me well – how can you tell?

When you came into my world, I stumbled. I fell.

I could feel my heart swell.

You rang within me like a bell.

It took some time before I got see

You were getting ready to flee.

I captured your poison in my grip;

It was easy to tear apart, easy to rip.

Your poison was never meant to complete its trip.

It began to lose its battle.

Did you really think I'd let it burn, let it settle?

Don't leave yet. You're finally caught in my net.

Stay here. I am not done.

It is too late to run.

I don't know why I let you in.

Perhaps it was your bright eyes, your confident grin?

You made me think that I had no options left.

You stole my choices. It was a bitter theft.

You were so gentle, so deft.

I shall do what I must.

You take over … then leave behind a pile of dust.

I was still a fighter, free of rust.

I mistook your passion for something more.

Now you're standing at my door.

Life cannot be walked alone.

Your poison penetrated my heart, my bone.

You had every right to live, to strive.

I taught you to swim, to dive.

I was not your puppet. I was alive.

Bit by bit, you took over every day.

You faced much resistance, much delay.

You didn't get to win; you didn't get to play.

In the end your poison was weak.

Things for you now look bleak.

You were never meant to stay.

I was not so easy to defeat, to slay.

ROSES

Layer upon layer of gleaming petal,

It is something to behold when the petals settle.

When the rose begins to wilt,

When its stem begins to tilt,

It starts to lose its beauty.

To shine is every rose's duty.

Light as a snowflake, a rose stands straight, stands tall.

It gives its all.

Its splendour isn't timeless. At some point, the petals begin to fall.

Fragrance so wholesome, lending fire to passion, to desire.

Roses are a symbol of love and empathy, grief and ire.

When the petals fly with the breeze, they enjoy their flight with ease.

The petals shrivel in the heat; in the winter, they freeze.

Roses are moody. They are difficult to nurture, to please.

Roses do not tolerate a rough hand,

They look good on water, on sand.

Roses can be intoxicating.

Anyone can fall victim to their thrall, their charm.

To feel the touch of a rose, one would gladly extend their hand, their arm.

Roses are grown everywhere, be it a home, or a farm.

They can calm the heart when it thuds in alarm.

Roses are gentle. They mean no harm.

A rose makes a great gift.

It gives the soul a lovely lift.

Roses are exquisite. They come at a hefty price.

Roses come with thorns. They are not always nice.

Roses can be soft as silk or sharp as ice.

Roses are greedy for affection and care.

They have no concept of sacrifice.

Roses can quickly learn to attract, to entice.

Roses are loved by the humble, the wise.

When it comes to a rose, don't judge it by its size.

A rose cannot be copied. Cannot be made.

With the passage of time, a rose begins to fade.

Roses are lovely;

No matter where they stand, they sit.

They belong everywhere. They always fit.

HOPE

I drown in my hope.

In my dreams I hang on to a longer rope.

It's all nice and comfortable.

I'm always steady; I am always ready.

My past is on the mend.

I am my own friend.

All roads lead to the same end.

I drown in my buoyancy as I cling to hope.

No matter what happens, I'm always ready to face it.

I am always ready to cope.

It all comes down to hope.

The evenings are shy,

But the day is an ally and I befriend it with ease,

All my hopes find a release.

Even amidst war, I search for peace.

DROWNING

You pull me under.

I'm drowning.

Can't you see?

If you cared, you'd set me free.

But I'm still trapped here in this endless sea.

Could it have been different between you and me?

Where equality ruled us; no buts or nos.

I sense a change; look – I'm still floating.

Still breathing.

It's not too late.

There is still time for pondering.

Don't look at me. I'm done pleading

And yet, I sense your refusal.

If that's so, then this is it.

I just wanted your acknowledgement.

This was never meant to be.

I shall no longer drown in this sea.

SACRIFICE

I was never afraid of a challenge.
I have faced vast oceans and violent winds,
Battled both fire and ice;
Nothing could prepare me for your ardour.
Your sacrifice.
Our past was filled with lies;
Despite this, you still honoured our ties.
I understand this now. My heart cries.
Had I known all that you sacrificed,
All that you left behind,
I would have been more understanding,
More kind.
A real sacrifice is difficult to witness, to find.
How could I have been so negligent?
So blind?
This is tearing me apart.
It is time to surrender, to do my duty,
To play my part.
You own my heart.
May we begin with a new slate?
It can't be too late.
We deserve another chance, another try,
This sea of lies has finally run dry.

I wish to laugh, to cry.

I wish to land, to fly.

Your sacrifice is a burden, a gift.

It brings me down, it gives me a lift.

Let us begin anew,

Our worries shall be few.

All our troubles shall vanish.

In the end, our doubts shall perish.

You are someone I would always honour,

Always cherish.

I will follow you with determination, night and day.

Let your sacrifice lead the way.

This is all I have to say.

WIND

The wind speaks of many secrets,

Long forgotten words of wisdom and sorrow,

Of topics both broad and narrow,

Of lands high and low,

Of seas deep and shallow,

Of ages dark and bright

And of burdens heavy and light.

Oh yes, the winds carry many secrets, but not for us.

How can I shift with the winds if I don't understand?

I stood up and took a stand.

The winds carry whispers, surrounding me, whispering and speaking.

My mind left my body far behind, listening,

Looking for an answer that will never come,

For why we are what we've become.

The winds shifted, looking for a new direction,

So did I, much to my exasperation.

Many have tried before me.

Many will try after me,

But none will succeed in this conquest.

The secrets will forever rest.

And the winds, guardians of said secrets, will

forever guard in their slumber,

Regardless of their rising number.

Until the secrets are ready to wake and to face us,

We wait.

As we have realized a fact quite sublime,

That in the end the key to unlock these secrets is

Time.

FACTS

When the world awakens,

Peace goes to sleep.

When our heart is awake,

The soul weeps.

When the sun shines, the light reigns.

When clouds gather, it rains.

When you look into the mirror,

It is your reflection you see.

To travel the world, you must cross the sea.

When it is hot, it is heat you feel.

There isn't much the balm of time can't heal.

For every occurrence there is consequence.

To everything, there is a sequence.

Cause and effect: Facts leading to facts.

DEAR DAD

I dedicate this poem to my father

You have always been there.

There is nothing you can't do, nothing you can't bear.

You know us. You care.

You taught us how to share.

We do our best to make you proud.

You showed us the moon when stars hid behind the cloud.

You can be silent; you can be loud.

Dear dad,

You taught us to aim straight, aim high.

We learned how to walk, how to fly.

You always know when we're sly,

When we lie.

With your support, we thrive;

We try.

Seas are no longer wet; deserts are no longer dry.

Our hardships lose their way; they pass us by.

Dear dad,

There is little you'd refuse us.

You show such patience when we begin to fuss.

When it comes to your family, there is nothing you'd deny,

Nothing you'd rebuff.

You are kind; you are tough.

You see right through us; you can easily call our bluff.

You always made sure we had plenty, that we'd had enough.

You show strength and courage when things get bad.

You bring a smile to our faces when we're sad.

You know just what to do.

For that we are happy; we are glad.

Remember the time when every day was a battle?

When it was difficult to land, to settle?

When we were so little, nothing made sense.

You always came to our defence.

You calmed us when we got tense.

You taught us to see beyond the smoke when it got dense.

Dear dad,

From you we have much to gain, much to learn.

We learn something new from you at every turn.

You are generous; you are stern.

Because of you, we know the difference between what is wrong

And what is right,

When to give in and when to fight.

According to you, the dark always gives way to light.

You can make even the shadows seem fascinating,

Seem bright.

You were there when we had our first nightmare,

Our first fright.

You taught us to be valiant, to do what is right.

We stopped fearing the dark, the night.

We can climb any height.

Dear dad,

It was you who taught us to ride a bike.

You encouraged us to try things we hate, we like.

You always stand by our side. Help us take it all in stride.

Dad, there is nothing we can't achieve when we work together.

You give weight to feather.

You never say never.

There is nothing that you'd run from,

Not now, not ever.

You are the best in your field.

People listen to you without question.

They follow; they yield.

Our whole life, you've been our shield.

We see our world through your eyes.

Finally, we get to see the difference between the truth,

The lies.

Dear dad,

When it rains, you become our shelter,

You take us under your wing.

You take care of it all,

Of everything.

You take our pain away when our wounds begin to sting.

We look forward to it all, no matter what the future shall bring.

You show us what it means to be tall.

You are there to catch us should we fall.

You have never ignored our call.

Your words are wise.

They make our hearts swell.

You are there to make sure our fears don't stay.

That they don't dwell.

No matter what happens, we know you mean well.

After all, whatever may happen, only time can tell.

You can always tell when we're ill, when we're unwell.

You were there for us, when we rose, when we fell.

Dear dad,

We remember the time when the world was new,

When it was frightening.

The truth struck like lightening.

There was so much light!

The world was a vast, magnificent sight.

It was the time when we learned to share, to fight.

Our doubts become few. They became slight.

You know what we feel.

Our wounds begin to heal.

You are always near.

You make things simple and clear.

You take away our fear.

You help us get to the top.

Taught us how to pull back, how to stop.

You help us reach our dreams.

We have strength to carry on,

No matter how difficult it seems.

You make our troubles disappear.

You know what to do when our doubts begin to appear.

You push us when we begin to slack.

You forgive us for all that we lack.

You taught us the difference between grey and black.

You always know where to find us when we hide.

You teach us to concentrate on what matters,

Put the rest aside.

Dear dad,

When it begins to snow, when it begins to rain,

You are always there for us when things begin to strain.

Our doubts and fear lose their edge.

They look simple and plain.

You showed us how to learn, how to train.

You make our thoughts take root;

You help them flow.

You encourage us to move quickly, to take it slow.

Because of you, we learned to let go of our past.

We run slow, run fast.

We can now make our happiness stay a while,

Make it last.

When things begin to change,

You make it look less strange.

To you, we are much like an open book.

You helped us be brave, no matter what it took.

You can always tell when something is wrong with a single look.

Your words can be calm, can be curt.

You always know when we are sad, when we are hurt.

When the snow becomes thick, when we become sick,

When the rain refuses to fade,

You become our shade.

You can always find a solution, a way.

You are there for your family,

Every day.

LAUGHTER

Laughter brings joy in life;
It is what blunts the edges of a knife.
Some people laugh to hide their true intention;
Some laugh to eradicate tension.
Some people laugh for show;
It brings the soul to a new low.
Laughter comes from within, from the heart.
Laughter is art.
Laughter can help when things go from worse to worst:
Much like a bubble, all dreams and hopes burst.
Laughter is like a sitting cloud.
It lifts the heart, makes one proud.
Laughter is quick; it doesn't dawdle behind.
Laughter is not something someone should mind.
Laughter is easy to find.
Laughter is without bounds;
It makes rounds.
Laughter cannot be controlled or be ruled.
Laughter cannot be fooled.
Laughter is easily available,
It is something of which everyone is capable.
Laughter is common;
There is plenty to go around.

Laughter is a magnificent sound.

Laughter can leave behind echoes of warmth and life,

Of times both joyful and glorious.

Laughter is not just for the victorious.

Generous, Laughter visits us all;

With its boisterous force, it can strike down any wall.

Between melancholy and laughter, it is the latter which stands tall.

Laughter can be unexpected,

It should always be respected.

Laughter cannot live in a cage.

Laughter knows no age.

Laughter can be locked away between the gum, the teeth.

It becomes difficult to know what lies beneath.

Laughter is unafraid of judgment.

Laughter needs no change, no adjustment.

Laughter cannot be taught;

It should not be fought.

Laughter cannot be borrowed, cannot be bought.

Laughter is a precious gift.

Laughter can be long or swift.

It elevates us all, gives us a lift.

Laughter can be quiet or loud.

It can draw a crowd.

Laughter is blind to poverty or wealth.

Laughter is great for health.

Laughter can be filled with malicious intent.

Laughter is strong;

It cannot be bent.

Laughter cannot erase pain, but it can make it bearable.

Laughter is the comfortable dress that is always wearable.

Laughter comes from within, but where does it go?

Laughter has no speed;

It is neither fast nor slow.

Laughter cannot whine;

It makes the eyes shine.

Laughter leads the soul to delight,

To brilliant light;

Laughter is a beautiful sight.

Laughter can win over any doubt;

Underestimated, laughter has a great deal of clout.

Laughter can soften any hurt, any fall.

Laughter answers the heart's call.

Laughter is invited to every party;

It is always sweet, never salty.

Laughter celebrates every occasion.

Laughter is never open to assault,

To invasion.

Unlike repressed emotion, laughter represents passion.

Laughter is forever ready; it needs no session.

It never goes out of fashion.

Laughter cures heartache.

Laughter should be done for laughter's sake.

Laughter can jolt a slumbering heart awake.

Laughter shields us from harsh truths, from bitter woes.

What the future brings … who knows?

Laughter is like chance:

It is an opportunity for the heart to dance.

Laughter needs no sense;

Laughter can be shallow or dense.

Laughter can be inappropriate, and cause a scandal.

Laughter is like the flame of a candle.

Laughter is something we all can handle.

Laughter is plentiful like sand.

Laughter cannot be banned.

Laughter is found in every race.

Laughter has lived on every continent,

Every city, every face.

Laughter can easily break;

It is not something someone can take.

Every ounce of laughter is incredible.

Laughter is never in vain; it can never be slain.

In the middle of a drought, laughter brings rain.

The power of laughter is ancient and certain.

Laughter hides behind no curtain.

Laughter cannot be beaten;

It cannot be eaten.

The power to laugh is the power to trust.

As ancient as laughter is, it knows no disease,

No rust.

Laughter puts everyone at ease.

To laugh, one doesn't need to be free.

Laughter is natural, like a tree.

It requires no hatred, no affection.

Those who want to laugh can easily find it within themselves;

They need no direction.

Laughter has no barrier.

It needs no language,

No specific age.

Laughter is found everywhere.

But beware!

Most contagious, Laughter is in the air.

Don't fear.

Laughter is innocent and harmless,

Like a drop of tear.

A champion of the oceans, no matter what the occasion is,

Laughter can always sail.

Laughter does not wail.

It will never disappoint, never fail.

Laughter laughs along when great stories are told.

Laughter should not be put on hold.

Laughter belongs to the sharp and the naïve.

Laughter makes one feel alive.

Laughter can be blunt and can be bold.

Laughter takes to laughing.

It doesn't need to be told.

In the face of misery, Laughter will never fold,

Laughter never grows old.

Laughter can never be a crime.

Laughter can be crooked or straight.

Laughter can be on time, or late.

Laughter is a hopeful sound.

Whenever one is lost, Laughter can be found.

WOMAN

Women are like water:

Plentiful, yet each drop is precious.

They can be compliant; they can be tenacious.

Women and water are signs of life;

Woman gives birth to life; water helps sustain it.

Without the other, neither can go on.

Soft and warm, or harsh as ice,

Women are known to be logical, to be wise.

Do not be deceived by their small size.

They favour the brutal truth over comforting lies.

They have it in them to rise above it all.

They can climb all walls,

Survive all falls.

CHANGE

I invite all that comes with change,

No matter if it is normal or strange.

I am always ready to increase my range.

Change is inevitable in life.

It can be soft or hard,

Or sharp as a knife.

Changes are blind to our feelings and emotion.

Change can cause a great deal of commotion.

Sometimes we resist change, make a stand.

Change is ignorant of it all; it cannot understand.

Some changes are gradual;

Some are manual.

Some changes are good for us;

We go for them without fuss.

Some changes can be heavy;

They can weigh a ton.

Some are mellow or as dazzling as the sun.

Change can be accepted or rejected without reason.

Change comes with every season.

Changes are not something from which one can run.

Some changes are not necessary;

They are simply done for fun.

Some changes are suspicious.

Some changes are inconspicuous.

Changes can be wrong or right.

Change can be controlled,

Left loose or tight.

Change is sometimes met with a fight.

Changes can be harsh; they can be curt.

Changes can heal, or they can hurt.

Changes change with time.

They can distort a verse,

Alter its rhyme.

Changes can be small or play a major part.

Sometimes change can touch the heart.

HEALING

The power to heal is the power to assist life.

To heal, one has to walk on edge,

Balance it all on a narrow ledge.

Healing can be costly or part of charity.

Healing can provide hope and clarity.

It can be light as breeze;

Healing can come with ease.

The ability to heal comes with talent and knowledge.

Like a tree, it is an ability that grows with age.

Healing is free of judgment and rage.

Much like an empty island, healing is silent.

Healing is never violent.

Healing promotes goodwill and health.

This in turn leads to relief,

To wealth.

With the power of knowledge and clear intentions,

Nothing stops healing.

It is your best bet when the flesh is ailing.

Sometimes healing can disappoint, for it cannot always win.

To admit defeat is not a sin.

Healing comes with instructions;

They must be followed.

Healing can be bought or borrowed.

If one wants to avoid disaster, they must follow the proper sequence,

In the absence of which one must face bitter consequence.

Healing can help save sanity;

It can help humanity.

Healing is a valuable art that all respect and cherish.

Healing is a skill that shall live forever.

It shall never perish,

Ever.

RUSH

In a world so easy, so difficult,

In a race so meaningless,

In the midst of all that is deep, that is hollow,

How long does it take before we lose ourselves?

You can either lead or follow.

Surviving in this world requires so much.

So many things we must do.

Things we fear, we must do too.

Sick of the routine,

We just want to be seen.

We crave adventure, the unknown.

But no one wants this alone.

Eyes set on the distant horizon,

We don't see what is placed right before us.

Much like a painter who cannot see past their brush,

We are always in such hurry to see things through.

Always in such a rush …

DOUBTS

He talks sweet to me,

But it's the same no more.

Maybe it's all just a lie my heart can't deny.

Did it all change overnight or was the change more gradual?

Funny how for things like this, we don't get a freaking manual.

In an attempt to keep things real, it became so cold,

So fake.

It's when you try so hard to make it work,

That it becomes difficult to take!

Perhaps the trick was to just let it flow?

Not worry about what's high or low?

Maybe we should've just tried harder.

Things then would have been better,

Right?

But of one thing I'm sure:

That I dream of you at night.

I feel happy; I feel light.

Perhaps for now that is enough?

Maybe it was never this tough.

So long as we have each other,

Everything will be fine.

All our warped doubts will walk a straight line.

ROAD

A road is something we all must take,

Sometimes shortly after we wake.

All roads lead to a destination.

No journey takes kindly to procrastination.

A means to an end, roads hold no fascination.

A road is no place for distraction.

Every journey begins with taking a road,

Except on water. where one must surrender to a boat.

A road can be tricky, or incomplete.

When on road, watch your speed!

On road, it is easy to follow,

Easy to lead.

Roads are easy to conquer,

Easy to beat!

Roads can be uncertain too.

Sometimes we end up lost:

If you wish to be found,

Turn around.

A road is what you make it to be.

Unlike our destination, a road is easier to see.

Roads are predictable; they host no mystery.

Roads are part of our future,

Our history.

A road cannot tell you where to turn,

Where to go …

Roads can take you high,

Take you low.

A road can be surrounded by darkness or bathed in the moon's glow.

Every road follows its own flow.

When on a road, you can go fast or you can go slow.

So go on: take a chance! Take a road!

See where it shall end;

Go see what lies round the bend!

SAME

I want my weakness to stay.

When all else fails, what else reminds you of your humanity?

When you begin to rise,

What else makes you fall?

It hurts, to look down always, when you are so tall.

Weakness is my balm: when I fall the pain goes away.

I look up to find myself a new way.

No more silence, no more fame.

If only all else falls too,

We'd finally all be same.

CONTROL

Control plays a controlling role.

Control can tame the soul.

Control is not for everyone.

It can be mellow, or bright as sun.

Control limits fun.

Control is priceless.

It cannot be bought; it cannot be won.

Control promises predictability.

Sometimes control is beyond one's ability.

Control stops the soul from corruption.

Control is averse to disruption.

When reality crumbles,

When the heart rumbles,

Control remains the only option.

Control keeps strong in the face of threats.

Control is something a lost soul dreads.

Control leaves lasting impression.

Control can defeat depression.

Control can falter; it can be lost.

The lack of control can deliver a heavy cost.

Control becomes better with experience, with age.

Control is strong;

It can vanquish rage.

Control can be demanding and can be wrong.

Control can be short-lived;

It can live long.

Control works alone; it cannot be ruled.

Control cannot be fooled.

Control is cold; it is well admired.

Control is not always desired.

Control is immune to affection.

Control doesn't promise perfection.

Control comes from within.

Control is ancient; it has always been there.

Control withers without care.

Control can soften a fall.

Careful control can break down any wall.

In the face of disaster, control stands tall.

Control answers a heart's call.

Control comes in useful when things begin to unravel.

Control can easily travel.

Control has lived in every city, every town.

Control tries not to let one down.

Control has always been around;

Control can be sharp or round.

It lives beneath the surface; it can always be found.

THE END?
OR THE BEGINNING?

This must be the beginning.

I have said goodbye to the end.

It is time to move again.

New things to gain,

Look forward to a bright future.

Past was spent in vain;

This must be the beginning.

I don't know where to start.

My mind is finally listening to my heart.

For better or worse, I welcome this new beginning,

Much like afternoon greets its beloved evening.

GREED

How can you define greed in a world filled with unnecessary goods,

When your needs exceed your wants?

Whether you are rich or poor, you are subjected to taunts,

For having too much or not enough,

For having it easy or tough.

When it's in our nature to reach for more than we can grasp,

When we continue using items, long after they last?

When the world stops, we search for the light.

No matter what happens, we are never averse to a beautiful sight.

In a world filled with falseness, we all want to be right.

How can you define greed, when having it better becomes your right?

Is it really greed when your wants exceed your needs?

Couldn't a large garden want more seeds?

STARS

Visible to the eye, yet so far out of reach,

The magnificence of stars is not something one can duplicate,

Someone can teach.

Touching the stars is a barrier one has yet to breach.

Ethereal and dazzling, their beauty is ancient and brutal.

When the nights are dark, when the moon is

concealed away, stars become vital.

Night and day, their light remains a constant in this dynamic world.

It never fades.

Stars come in many shades.

As they hover, weightless and proud,

Stars are as enticing to look at as the moon next to a cloud.

SUGAR

Sugar is the spice of life.

To cut through it, one doesn't require a knife.

Sugar can be warm and cold.

Sugar can be new and old.

Sugar can be shy or bold.

Total opposites, sugar and salt are best friends.

Popular by choice, they travel in all circles.

Forbidden to some, sugar and salt defy all rules.

They are every chef's favourite tools.

Sugar can fix anything,

Make something out of nothing.

Sugar is sweet and delectable.

Sugar is safe and predictable.

Sugar can be white or brown.

It is every dessert's crown.

THE ELUSIVE SEARCH
FOR WORDS

One always searches for the right words to say,

The right words can make or break your day.

They can help you reach your goal, your way.

Words can be heard, can be understood,

Words can move you from where you once stood.

Words help us get closer to the truth.

For something so little, so much is lost.

Words carry a heavy cost.

Could the right words save you?

Words hold power, or so we're told.

Words can be new or old.

Words carry age, and hold wisdom.

Words can free your soul;

Words can lead to freedom.

DREAMS OF GRANDEUR

Let's sow these dreams of grandeur.

Under the light of sun, let us watch the seeds grow into a tree.

Not long now, our dreams can finally be free.

Having spent too long in the confines of our minds,

They can still shine.

Like their hosts, dreams too can whine.

There's no running from what lives within.

Dreams haunt you, eager to begin.

How do you handle that which is uncontrollable?

Some dreams are born from hidden desire;

They are blind to love and ire.

Like a horse without reins, dreams cannot be conquered.

A leader from inception, dreams are meant to be followed.

They can only be created, never borrowed.

Dreams can make you run, make you stop,

They come to all, be it a criminal or a cop.

Dreams come at night, but they don't mind stealing your sleep.

Dreams can be both shallow and deep.

Dreams can destroy your peace.

Dreams can rip you apart piece by piece.

Dream is a destination that can always be reached.

It's a fortress that can never be breached.

Dreams can bring light when you are surrounded by shadows.

Dreams are powerful; they can chase away your sorrows.

Dreams are essential in life.

So dream on! Dream for a dream.

After all, what is tea without cream?

PAIN

If pain can be conquered,

Then why suffer alone?

Pain torments the flesh, the bone.

It is nothing compared to the ailment of the heart, the soul.

Pain plays a painful role.

Pain is a war we must fight; we must survive.

Pain makes us feel alive.

If life were a book, pain would be the words on it.

Alongside joy, pain fights for dominance.

In our lives, both are strong in their prominence.

Pain is a harsh enemy.

It comes without warning and aims to destroy,

Much like a child tosses aside a broken toy.

Pain can be minuscule, or it can take over the senses.

Pain can break fences.

Pain makes us grit our teeth; it makes our eyes blurry.

Pain is as peculiar as a seed in a berry.

Pain is a rocky ocean;

It can sink a ferry.

Pain can be quiet.

It can cause a riot.

Pain can come as a song.

Pain can also come with a wound,

Be it wide or long.

To bear pain, one needs to be strong.

Pain is oblivious to what is right, what is wrong.

Pain can be shallow,

Make the soul wallow.

Pain can touch the heart.

It can be as astringent as tart.

If misery loves company, then what of pain?

With the dark cloud comes the rain.

Pain has nothing to gain;

It is never in vain.

Pain and misery are much like lovers.

No matter where they may go,

One will always find the other;

They are the two polar ends of the same tether.

They are cut from the same cloth.

Pain becomes worse with sloth.

If pressed, pain becomes stronger.

If ignored, it only stays longer.

Pain is uninvited, though it may become an expected

guest when certain trials come to pass.

Trying to shut your doors to it would be crass.

One way or another, pain shall arrive.

It never stops to strive,

Pain is like a vehicle we all must drive.

Pain can cause accidents,

Make you lose your way.

It becomes difficult to face the world, seize the day.

Pain is a reminder that things change all the time;

Nothing stays the same.

Pain reminds the beast what it means to be tame.

Pain is strong.

It can hurt, but that doesn't mean it's wrong.

Pain can serve as a warning;

It can let us know when we are wrong or lost.

Sometimes, pain comes at a high cost.

Pain is an enigma.

What does it mean when the soul aches?

What to do when the pain wakes?

If there was ever a cure to make pain slumber

forever, would we dare take it?

Uncover all of our defences, leave them naked?

Why would it be necessary, now that the enemy's conquered?

It is the promise of war that makes us strive for peace.

Pain is difficult to please.

Now that there's no more pain

Has all our previous suffering been for nothing?

Was it all in vain?

Pain is in the heart, the soul and the mind.

Pain is fairly easy to dodge, to find.

Pain is rarely kind.

Pain is always blind.

Pain is painful,

But it can sometimes come with a cure too.

It hurts when you disinfect a wound or two.

If joy is the sun in the sky, pain is the moon in the night.

Though it is hard to see when it's dark, it too carries light.

It makes you appreciate all things beautiful and bright.

Though it loves to play with us, pain is no lark.

It has an important role in our lives:

After all, what is light without the dark?

JOY

Birds chirping, children clapping, trees moving and the barley shaking:

That is *joy*.

Innocents laughing, no more lies:

That is *joy*.

The remorseful receiving forgiveness:

That is *joy*.

Moon glowing and sun shining, clouds drifting and winds shifting:

That is *joy*.

Birth of a child, a lifetime well-lived:

That is *joy*.

Don't ever let it be destroyed.

END

How do you know it is the end?

When the world has stopped spinning,

When the hearts stop winning?

When there is no more race?

When footprints disappear without a trace,

When you know everyone, every face?

When there is nothing new to understand, to learn,

When the trees no longer have branches,

When there are no more ferns?

When darkness is all you see?

When you have locked up your life and lost its key?

When bored and miserable is the way to be?

When your nights have become dreamless? Restless?

When ambition and success were met so long

ago, it is hard to tell when it all began.

When there is nowhere to go, to run?

When everywhere you go, all you see is the past?

Opportunities and hopes were once vast.

When everything is quick and nothing seems to last?

When seasons mesh together, is that the end?

When we are all genuine, we no longer pretend.

How do you know it is the end?

When love has conquered all or when hatred reigns supreme,

When the rules have changed so butter no longer makes cream.

When water avoids the stream?

When do you know it is the end?

When music meets barriers,

When oceans run dry,

When humans cease to cry?

It is the end when the heart forgets its beat,

It pumps hatred through the hollow flesh.

The good and the bad join hands,

They no longer clash.

When lightening has forgotten its flash?

It is the end when all trials are final,

When forgiveness is met with denial.

It is the end when all hurts are timeless,

When hope has lived a short life,

When cliffs have lost their depth.

Fate is decided on the edge of a knife.

LIES ARE DAY;
TRUTH IS NIGHT

I'm rising.

Don't trust them; they are lying.

I am not delusional; the truth is playing with you all,

A game called hide and seek.

Only the courageous find it,

Never the weak.

I'm rising.

The sun's no longer shining,

But the moon is glowing.

No more lying, the sun has chased it all away.

It is dark now, with only the truth left to show the way.

Speak softly; the truth shall hear the faintest sound.

Tread gently, the truth is temperamental,

Unafraid to strike you down.

Lies are gentle.

They coddle and comfort your soul.

Truth is harsh; it plays no such role.

When the sun is set,

Only truth can guide your way.

When the moon glows upon you,

Like the ocean, you must follow its sway.

HIDE

I follow this road, looking ahead.

This is where our chase has led.

Like the distant flap of wings, I hear echoes of your laughter,

Your smile.

I've been following you for a mile.

I hear you up ahead,

Walking alone, unafraid.

I hear your footsteps fade.

Your fragrance leads me to you like a moth to a flame,

I cannot ignore that call. I am not without blame.

I follow you like a soul follows its destiny, its heart.

My chase begins with a start;

You are the brush stroke of colour to my canvas of art.

I see you. You cannot hide.

For you, my eyes are wide.

I hear your laughter vanish as you turn round the corner,

Why hide when we both know how this will end?

One of us shall have to break this trend.

We are meant to be together.

This shall last forever.

I see you ahead of me, running away.

I'd chase you all the same,

Night and day.

What do you hear when I call for you?

Your name?

My voice?

It is your choice.

I will always run after you until one of us is caught;

This cannot be fought.

One day these games shall end.

All our burdens shall be light as a feather.

Things will be better.

One day, we shall be together.

DEAR BROTHER

I dedicate this poem to my brother

You were close by when I was born;
Your devotion was never split, never torn.
You shared your first toy with me.
You let me be.
Dear bro:
You were older than me. You were fast.
I never came last.
I remember it all. I have not forgotten the past.
You taught me how to keep my word.
I learned how to run like a horse, fly like a bird.
Every time I tumbled, I fell,
You were there to make sure I was well.
You helped me climb my first chair, my first tree.
I then learned when to fight and when to flee!
I no longer feared the open sea.
Dear bro:
You always have my back.
Thanks to you, I can let go; I can slack.
We told each other our secrets,
Shared our regrets, our fear.
You were always near.

You understood my words, loud and clear.

No argument in the world could ever drive us apart.

I still like sweet, and you still favour tart.

You learned how to cook, to show me your best dish.

You honour my request, my wish.

Dear bro:

We rarely ever like the same song,

Our fights are never mundane. They are never long.

You are protective when things fall apart, when they go wrong.

I appreciate your aid.

Your presence is always welcome, always great!

I remember the time when I broke something precious.

You were determined to keep my guilt at bay.

You were tenacious.

Dear bro:

You taught me the difference between honesty and pride.

You were always truthful with me. You never lied.

You were always good at putting a smile on my face.

You helped me win every challenge, every race.

There were times when I couldn't catch up, when I was slow.

You stopped. You paused. You helped things flow.

When you have my back, the wind is afraid to blow.

We protect one another from melancholy, from grief.

When the breeze hits, we follow one another like a broken leaf.

Dear bro:

You read me my first story.

When you did something wrong, you were quick to apologize.

You were sorry.

Your first gift to me was a book.

You can tell I'm hiding something with a single look.

You help me deal when life gets tough.

You let me know when enough is enough.

Sometimes, things get rough.

Dear bro:

I never doubted your compassion, your generosity.

There should be more people like you in every town, every city.

You are a genius. You are witty.

You taught me how to drive, how to strive.

I felt alive.

Whatever you learned, you taught me the same.

I can talk about everything with you.

No discussion is ever silly or lame.

Nothing can change your attitude towards me.

You are someone who would always treat me the same.

How you can quickly solve any issue will always remain a mystery.

I have always been amused that you hated math, but loved history.

You've always been great at controlling your anger, your rage.

You have always displayed strength and courage.

Dear bro:

You may be taller, but I am not small.

In life, we rise; we fall.

We cannot win it all.

You taught me to rise with grace.

I steadily hold on to my place.

We made jokes, pulled pranks.

We always stood by each other when we moved up the ranks.

Dear bro:

When things got bad,

You were there: for that I'm glad.

We were happy; we were sad.

Without you, life would've been boring and simple.

I remember you making fun of me when I got my first pimple.

Whenever things got crooked, you were there

to straighten out any dispute,

Any wrinkle.

You filled my life with fun and ease.

You were quick to comfort, quick to tease.

Dear bro:

You excel at every test.

You are the best.

You will always take my side.

Our foes better watch out.

They better hide.

Dear bro:

Thanks for everything thus far …

Mind if I take your car?

FACE IT ALL

Face it all:
The slow rise, the quick fall.
The good, the bad,
The loss of what we may have had.
Face the low and the high.
Face it all.
Just don't wonder why.
Better to be oblivious to the truth than nurture a lie.
There is nowhere to hide, to run.
Face the heat, the sun.
Soon, it shall all be done.
All battles shall cease; all shall be won.
Conquer or be conquered.
Face it all.
The cold beauty of winter, the soft whisper of fall:
Face their call.
Face the brittle words, the hard wall.
Face it all.
Stand tall;
Do your best,
Maybe then the soul can finally rest.
Fight for the victory that shall be sweet in the end.
All that you have faced shall begin to heal, to mend.
After a harrowing test,
Let us face satisfying slumber in the eternal nest.

DESPERATION

Desperation is unwelcome, yet all encompassing.

When desperation makes a home in your heart or your mind,

The world ceases to make sense, no matter what the eyes may find.

Desperation is never gentle, never kind.

It makes one blind.

When hope begins to wither, desperation begins to grow.

The blood freezes, it refuses to flow.

When the light remains elusive,

When nothing seems conclusive,

What power does desperation hold?

In the middle of winter, it leaves us cold.

Desperation divides.

Desperation unites.

Desperation lives under the surface,

Always ready to strike!

It makes us do things we despise. Things we don't like.

Desperation leaves one hollow.

When the night is dark, desperation is quick to follow.

FORGIVENESS

Forgiveness can put the mind, the soul at ease.

Forgiveness can give release.

It is easily spotted, easily seen.

There is so much forgiveness can mean.

The world is livelier where forgiveness has come to stay.

It is brighter than day.

When a guilty heart is filled with yearning,

Bright and peaceful, forgiveness comes every night, every morning.

Forgiveness follows no one's sway.

When the heart begin to ache, when the soul begins to wake,

Forgiveness is the cure, the way.

Forgiveness is always welcome, always accepted.

Yet forgiveness is seldom expected.

Forgiveness covers every aspect.

In every circle, forgiveness calls forth admiration and respect.

Individually tailored for each person, forgiveness is for all.

Aware of the deepest, darkest secrets, forgiveness does not judge.

Once it's given, it is yours. It cannot budge.

Forgiveness can make one soar; it can make the soul roar.

Forgiveness can touch the heart, the core.

Forgiveness shall sew up all that was once torn.

Forgiveness dwells out of sight; it cannot be worn.

Wherever it is desired, forgiveness is born,

Calm yet strong, forgiveness can never go wrong.

Forgiveness can be brief; it can be long.

The ability to forgive is for the truly strong.

Forgiveness is something we all at some point desire;

Something we all want and need.

When anger and rage make the heart and the soul weak,

Forgiveness is something one begins to seek.

It elevates hope, defeats all that remains bleak.

Forgiveness is distinct. It is unique.

Forgiveness has no conditions, no demands.

It easily makes amends.

Forgiveness is primordial. It is real.

Yet no matter what day it is, what age,

It is always ideal.

Spoken softly, the whisper of forgiveness carries.

It is precious, like fragile grapes and fresh berries.

Can forgiveness not be enough?

If given like a false gesture, has it lost all meaning?

All power?

Does it leave one marooned on the edge of a cliff,

On the top of a mountain, or a tower?

Doubts linger longer. Fear becomes stronger.

Even if slowly, forgiveness should be given completely.

It should be awarded wholly.

Sufferance is the result of anger and pain.

Forgiveness does not turn all hardships meaningless;

They were not in vain.

It is about more than just the loss, the gain.

We all make mistakes.

Forgiveness gives; it never takes.

After a long, dark journey it is forgiveness that lies at the end, in wait.

Forgiveness can carry any secret, regardless of its weight.

Forgiveness is the symbol of generosity.

Bright and certain, forgiveness lights up the soul with its luminosity.

Sometimes forgiveness is found in the eyes, without words,

Without a sound.

Peace and joy reign in the soul once forgiveness is achieved,

Once it has been found.

SLOW

Don't rush; take it easy.

Some things are best done slow.

Just keep it natural; just let it flow.

Let it be gentle; let it be slow.

Care demands time

Much like a poem expects rhyme.

Time waits for no one. Fighting it, nobody has ever won.

Lay back and let it all come to you.

Why bother, why run?

Let it be placid; let it be slow.

Don't worry about the high, the low.

Take a chance and measure your steps.

Look below.

Walk slow.

HUNGER

A wave of lethargy overtakes, just as the blood

rushes fiercely through the veins.

It is hard to control a horse without reins.

Hunger is deep and all encompassing.

With rise in conflicting emotions, one goal is clear:

That any sustenance, in any shape or form, would be held dear.

Hunger is not related to poverty.

It comes to us all.

Its grip is absolute; there is no escape from its growling call.

The belly becomes a beast;

One that craves a feast.

It can be put down with ease.

Hunger is a debilitating enemy.

It defeats many.

STAY WITH ME

My world has finally started to rotate, to spin.

I can now hear silence in this din.

There is little to lose;

There is plenty to choose.

The winds have decided to blow;

My thoughts have shifted direction. They have started to flow.

I am in the air. I now have wings!

Can't you hear my heart?

It sings!

Stay with me.

My past makes sense when you are here.

Riddles finally make sense. They become clear.

I am no longer afraid of fear.

Stay with me, my dear.

There is so much to hide, so much to say.

We are here to stay.

I know we are meant to be.

It is time for our doubts to flee!

Together we shall grow, much like a tree.

We have so much to look forward to,

So much to learn.

Together we fall; we burn.

We shall always be there for each other,

At every round, at every turn.

Things for us are about to change.

They shall be new. They shall be strange.

I know you shall remain here.

I want you close. I need you near.

If you stay, this night will turn into day.

Don't you see?

Together we should stay.

PROMISES

A promise is the closest thing to trust.

It is the only thing that stands tall when everything else begins to rust.

If trust were a mountain, it would be promise that sits atop.

Promise is akin to a large field, filled with potential crop.

A promise can be broken,

Given freely as a false token.

Promise stands alone and proud.

It can stand out in a crowd.

Promise can be uncertain;

No one knows what it will bring.

A promise can be strong;

It can encourage even the weakest of hearts to sing.

Promise follows wherever one goes,

Follows surreptitiously behind.

Nothing can shake it off:

No car, No train.

In the middle of a wasteland, promise can bring rain.

In a room filled with treasury trinkets, promises can make one feel hollow.

When a promise is broken, it leaves behind sorrow.

Promises can make the world shine,

Strengthen our defences,

And turn life sublime.

Promises can give false hope,

But even that is good enough on an uneven road.
Promises give strength to bear the heaviest load.
Promises should be given with care.
Wherever they go they leave behind a lair,
Filled with hope, aspirations and doubt.
No matter where they go,
Promises hold a great deal of clout.

VICTORY

Victory demands a hefty price.

It answers to truth. Not lies.

Sometimes victory takes too long to come.

Sometimes it leaves one numb.

Victory belongs to those who are honest and kind.

Victory isn't easy to find.

It is not something that can be bought.

Victory is free. It can never be captured, never be caught.

Victory comes naturally, or doesn't come at all.

Victory moves from place to place, much like a ball.

Victory helps us stand tall.

To greet victory, one must learn to greet the morning,

The night.

Victory usually comes after a long, arduous fight.

Once the heart begins to mend,

The battle is at an end.

Victory makes a wonderful sight.

It comes down to greet us from a great height.

Victory reminds us of our past.

Victory is never meant to last.

Victory is neither forgiving nor is it cruel.

Victory follows only one rule:

It does not come to a fool.

For those of high calibre, victory is difficult to lose.

Between defeat and victory, the latter is easier to choose.

MASQUERADE

Image over image,

Mask over mask,

Have you forgotten who you are yet?

Eyes alight with betrayal, heart darker than your raven hair,

Your features – for your kind – so rare.

What does one look like when they have no care?

I feel your eyes on me as you continue to stare.

Once upon a time your gaze was difficult to bear.

Your mask became your door.

No more!

Do you not see all those masks tossed away?

Sitting in the dirt, night and day?

They are where they will stay.

Take off your mask.

It is not that hard a task.

Become who you were born to be.

Only then shall you last.

Look towards the future; forget about the past.

Slow down, you're going too fast.

Keep your head high; never let your principles bend.

A Masquerade too, like everything,

Shall one day end.

POVERTY

Ever heard of poverty? Isn't that a bitter reality?

Why is it that we turn our faces away from such horror, without remorse?

How can we not see when people suffer and turn morose?

There is only one way to battle this: forget a chocolate or a rose.

It doesn't even come close.

They need our support more than our concern,

Understanding their plight is something we must learn.

Let us share our wealth and care,

Make their reality easier to bear.

They just need a few things from us in a small dose.

Is it so hard to apply one of those?

With a little devotion and a little money,

We could come up with a solution that would help so many.

AFRAID

Are you afraid of the approaching disaster, where the hour
draws closer and the icy tendrils of fear grow denser?
When the storm rides on the back of the night
It makes a formidable sight.
Are you afraid of the doom that will follow?
For surely, life can be shallow.
Are you afraid there will only be regret and sorrow,
The dawn of light so hollow, like there'll never be a tomorrow?
Are you afraid?
Yes? Me too.
Let us then run, side by side, hand in hand,
To a place where darkness cannot follow.
For every fool has a right to hope, if our circumstances can allow.
And the right time to run is now!
Thunder cracks the vast sky.
Look out!
Here comes the shadow.
It may appear to be so mellow.
But do not be deceived,
For any escape from it will likely be narrow.

DO YOU HAVE
WHAT IT TAKES?

Do you have what it takes to learn?

Do you have what it takes to burn?

Do you have what it takes to fight battles unknown?

Do you have what it takes to venture out in the darkness alone?

Do you have what it takes to protect your own?

Do you have what it takes to hold onto your belief?

Do you have what it takes to give relief?

Do you have what it takes to keep the darkness at bay?

Do you have what it takes to stay?

Do you have what it takes to trust?

Do you have what it takes to expunge the rust?

Do you have what it takes to work through the dust?

Do you have what it takes to clean up someone's mess?

Do you have what it takes to work with less?

Do you have what it takes to work under stress?

Do you have what it takes to confess?

Do you have what it takes to fly?

Do you have what it takes to tell a lie?

Do you have what it takes to refuse, to deny?

Do you have what it takes to fall?

Do you have what it takes to conquer all?

Do you have what it takes to rise?

Do you have what it takes to judge by size?

Do you have what it takes to fight?

Do you have what it takes to hold on tight?

Do you have what it takes to face the night?

Do you have what it takes to bite?

Do you have what it takes to see the light?

Do you have what it takes to hold power in the palm of your hand?

Do you have the power to take a stand?

Do you have what it takes to add flavour to something bland?

Do you have what it takes to keep enemies close?

Do you have what it takes to see past your own nose?

Do you have what it takes to care for the ill?

Do you have what it takes to control your will?

Do you have what it takes to avoid desire?

Do you have what it takes to put out the fire?

Do you have what it takes to stand tall, when situations turn dire?

Do you have what it takes to fly higher?

Do you have what it takes to let go?

Do you have what it takes to say no?

Do you have it takes to agree?

Do you have what it takes to nurture a tree?

Do you have what it takes to walk on a busy road?

Do you have what it takes to carry a heavy load?

Do you have what it takes to earn love?

Do you have what it takes to care for a dove?

Do you have what it takes to ignore a simple shove?

Do you have it takes to say enough?

Do you have what it takes to sort through the stuff?

Do you have what it takes to hold back when you have ample?

Do you have what it takes to keep things simple?

Do you have what it takes to play by the rule?

Do you have what it takes to win a duel?

Do you have what it takes to suffer through pain?

Do you have what it takes to refrain?

Do you have what it takes to honour someone brave?

Do you have what it takes to behave?

Do you have what it takes to chase your dream?

Do you have what it takes to look past the gleam?

Do you have what it takes to catch fish in a stream?

Do you have what it takes to ignore?

Do you have what it takes to answer the door?

Do you have what it takes to open your heart?

Do you have what it takes to appreciate art?

Do you have what it takes to face your past?

Do you have what it takes to last?

Do you have what it takes to do something right?

Do you have what it takes to avoid a fight?

Do you have what it takes to survive a fright?

Do you have what it takes to continue when things get trite?

Do you have what it takes to face your fear?

Do you have what it takes to keep your mind clear?

Do you have what it takes to protect those you hold dear?

Do you have what it takes to forgive?

Do you have what it takes to *live*?

MEMORIES

I remember the time when we first met:

The weather was a bit cold, a bit wet.

The moon shone in all its unbound glory,

And so began our story.

The next time we met, the day was dark and dreary.

We were a bit tired, a bit weary.

The day after that, our paths became one.

We lost. We won.

The following day, the world seemed so wrong,

So right.

You were a wonderful sight,

Your words so strong, so kind;

People like you are difficult to find.

You always knew what to do, what to say.

You'd mould me like clay.

I see you when I close my eyes.

You know all my secrets, all my lies.

You are always there when my heart cries.

You are the reason I choose to be more.

You live within my core.

When you're upset, when you're about to bolt,

My heart breaks. My soul grinds to a halt.

You are both my sugar and my salt.

My sorrow is never your fault.

How do you know when I'm far away?

When I need you straightaway?

Our hearts are joined.

They beat together.

Can you hear me when I think your name?

Our doubts, once strong and wild –

Are they now tame?

With you, I belong.

So tell me:

What took you so long?

TELL ME

When was the last time you saw the light of day?

Tell me.

When was the last time you had something to say?

Tell me.

Did you listen to the whispers in the night?

Tell me.

Did you ever walk away from a fight?

Tell me.

Did you ever push too hard when chances for success were slight?

Tell me.

Did you ever let go of your illusions?

Tell me.

Did you give in to your delusions?

Tell me.

Have you ever tasted too much salt?

Tell me.

Has everything been my fault?

Tell me.

Why you refused to stay the same?

Why you'd always change?

Was it for me?

Was I your sea, vast and deep?

You were always afraid to swim.

Is that why you'd change every day on a whim?

Tell me about your fears.

Tell me. I want to understand the reason behind your tears.

Am I sitting too far, too high?

Did you think I didn't care?

That I wouldn't be just, or fair?

I reached you, time and again.

It had all been in vain.

You turned away without words.

Suddenly our nest was empty, without birds.

I heard you were difficult, that you were cold.

It didn't matter to me. I was bold.

You brought your past into your present.

Let me tell you:

It wasn't pleasant.

Now I see you, reformed and sad.

You miss what we had.

You want another go at this, another chance.

Somewhere the music's playing again. I can see you wish to dance.

I smile and wait for your glance.

I am glad you have finally accepted yourself,

that you've finally taken a stance.

Tell me.

What does it feel like to look into the mirror and like what you see?

Now that your doubts and insecurities have vanished,

Tell me, do you finally feel free?

To you, my window is always open.

From you, I need no gift, no token.

Tell me.

Do you feel the difference now that you're finally whole?

Finally complete?

Tell me: when do you want to start over and meet?

DON'T LOOK BACK

Don't look back, or else you'll stay.

There are monsters up ahead which you must slay.

If you stay, the night shall become day.

But only for a moment, the rest shall face delay.

Don't look back.

Your past comes to knock on your door.

If you stay, it'll travel deep into your core.

Don't look back.

The future has much in store.

If you stay, you shall have to fix all that you destroyed.

Everything you tore.

Don't look back. You must move on.

Forget about the dusk. Look towards the dawn.

Don't look back.

What of those who need you to move on?

Could you leave them to their fate?

Can they afford for you to be late?

Forget about the past. Begin with a new slate.

This choice between your heart and your soul is challenging indeed.

In the end, it is the heart that is forced to bleed.

When one can help, why allow suffering?

Why not stop, change things that are differing?

Don't look back. Just leave. Just go away.

Who knows? Perhaps you shall be back one day.

PASSION

It's been so long since the world understood my language.

We are no longer on the same page.

Can't do anything about it at this stage.

I changed yet remained the same.

I remained true to myself.

I ignored both wealth and fame.

Passion demands both devotion and sacrifice.

Life without passion is like food without spice.

I am happy where I am. It will have to suffice.

I have an idea, a vision.

I don't need to fit in. I need no supervision.

It will only lead to confusion and division.

This situation is hard, yet I'd have it no other way.

This is the way I'll stay.

I have much to give this way.

THREAD

I hang by a strong thread, one you wove with your lies.

I hold onto it while I stare into your eyes.

I watch in fascination as the emotions swirl in them.

Do you have any idea what I see in them?

How much they speak to me?

The words you don't say to me, but those that I can clearly see?

Now that I know, how can I let it be?

If betrayal it is you have in your eyes, your heart,

Then behold as I play my part.

I throw my own dice.

The question burns in your eyes.

What say the dice?

But it's too far down below.

One of us will have to let go.

Don't worry, for I will retrieve it for you.

Take back this thread.

For I'm letting go of this.

It's a pity we won't ever see each other again,

That in the end, all our efforts were in vain.

Oh, how I wished to tell you that the dice were plain …

A PERFECT DAY

It was a beautiful morning.

The sun shone; the clouds played hide and seek;

Every good thing had reached a peak.

It was a day of such luck.

For many it was the perfect day to take the leap.

A day for the strong,

Not the weak.

It was the perfect day to relax and hit the lake.

No giving, it was the time to take.

It was perfect.

There was no one to blame.

A perfect day, a perfect moment:

Pity how they are so rare.

Perhaps that's why, when they finally come around,

We actually *care*.

ICE

Ice is the opposite of fire.

Losing this precious commodity would lead to

consequences both harsh and dire.

Weary of battle, ice shall begin to tire.

Nature will then take over. Show us her ire.

Ice means us no harm.

Its destruction is cause for alarm.

When the forces of smoke begin to gather,

Ice begins to melt.

It's a change that is keenly felt.

Ice has no scent, no taste.

Ice is so easy to waste.

Ice is not something one can construct.

It is not something one can control, one can instruct.

Surrounded by heat, ice is a wonderful surprise.

Ice knows how to fall, how to rise.

When it comes to ice, do not judge it by its size.

Ice is neither foolish nor wise.

Ice makes a powerful friend, a vicious foe.

The formation of ice takes time. It is slow.

Much like fire, ice too can burn.

Ice is necessary for survival, at every corner, every turn.

Ice never sinks; it quickly learns to swim.

It floats close to the rim.

Ice has more than one use.

It isn't something we can afford to lose.

FIRE

You pull me closer.

I can't breathe as it grows darker, denser.

I cough; I choke.

Your ember eyes smoulder with their burning gaze.

I can feel I'm losing myself in this endless haze.

I look for an escape, but I can find none in this confusing maze.

If only I could concentrate, I know there are ways.

No matter what my courage stays.

Heat and smoke became my walls.

If these walls couldn't stop others from entering, how could they keep someone in!

Despite the rising dust and the scorching heat, there has to be a way out,

A way to win!

If it were water I would take a swim.

But what of fire,

Which destroys at whim?

This has reached its brim.

Like a wave of a tsunami, this fire rises taller.

To survive it, I will have to be stronger.

How long has it been thus far?

A day? An eternity?

Does this fire have no end, no dignity?

Rather than receding, it continues to devour,

It continues to grow larger by the hour.
To bring this down I have to strike much lower.
I push on as water fuels its dying ire.
When it comes to the real thing, you can't beat fire with fire.

SWEPT AWAY

I am floating in this sea of doubt and love.

The waves carry me about with such delicate care.

It is becoming easier to bear.

With your presence beside me, my pain is washed away.

I fear no more.

Even when drowning, I can feel my spirit soar.

This sea has me surrounded from all sides,

Like a rag doll, I am subjected to its relentless tides.

Getting away from it all only pulls me in deeper.

I no longer know my way. I have no sense of time or day.

With you beside me, I have suffered this

ocean like a bird suffers its wings.

This is my choice.

So rejoice!

I don't regret everything I have left behind, all those things.

My soul drifts alongside of me,

A silent companion.

Sometimes it sings;

My trust in you is much like a flight of wings.

In this ocean of love and doubt, neither can live without the other.

They must remain together.

Love fuels doubt, and doubt feeds on love.

Neither suits the other, but they fit like a hand in a glove.

Take it away and this ocean is meaningless to me.

I need the day. I need the night.

I need the love. I need the doubt.

They say there can be no doubt where there is love.

How can courage survive without test, without fear?

You need weakness to remind you of strength,

Much like you need tape to measure length.

I have only two eyes,

One for love and one for doubt,

My heart is my own; it surrenders to no one's clout.

Together my eyes see the image in black and white.

I get to see what is wrong, what is right.

If you swim beside me for long, one day you too shall drown.

I know you'd do it with a grin, never a frown.

This ocean is all in my soul, my heart,

And you are the tide that keeps me afloat.

With you beside me, I need no raft, no boat.

For as long as we live in this ocean, we shall gladly swim.

Together, no future is grim.

HOME

In the end, when everything is said and done,

When everything's lost or won,

Home is where the heart is.

Home is where the soul goes.

Home is the remedy for all of life's woes.

Home is the answer to all of life's riddles.

Home is the pathway without pebbles.

Home is for the obedient, for the rebels.

Home is sweet;

It is neat.

Home is forgiving;

It can be giving.

Home is deep;

It is where one can peacefully sleep.

Home is where secrets can be safely stored.

Home can never be bored.

Home cannot travel;

Home can unravel.

Home is where the heart – the soul – rests.

Home is without trials, without tests.

Home brings peace.

Home puts everyone at ease.

Home is where charity can begin;

It is where love can win.

Home is free.

It is like a tree.

Home grows, its branches reaching out for generations;

Its leaves fall on domestic habitation.

Home is for the great.

Home is a place no one can rate.

Home is never a burden; it is always light.

Like reality, home can never bite.

Home is where the soul craves to sleep;

Home is where the strong break down to weep.

Home is where no one is last.

Home is vast.

Home is where your defences are best.

Home is where a warrior can rest.

Home is away from gossip, from scandal.

Home lights up with just a candle.

Home can be loose; can be tight.

Home is bright.

Home is where mysteries flourish, safe and sound.

Home is where it all goes round and round.

Home is addictive.

Home can never be vindictive.

Kind and understanding, it shall never judge.

Home's loyalty is absolute, it shall never budge.

Home is where the questions twirl.

Home is where the answers swirl.

Home can be up or down.

Home is found everywhere:

Every city, every town.

Home is where nothing can vanish.

Home is where no one shall be banished.

Home is without crowd.

Home can be silent or loud.

Home makes everyone proud.

Our way to home can never be lost.

Losing one's home is a terrible cost.

Home is where the family reunites;

Home is where the days are tranquil, and fun are the nights.

Home is where mornings are welcomed with baked foods.

Home is home.

It can be in the city or in the woods.

Home is where every ordeal becomes bearable.

Home is like an event where everything is wearable.

Home is like the calm before the storm.

Home is warm.

Home is like an everlasting star.

It feels close even when it is far.

Home is better than a great car.

Home has love deep within its riveting core.

Home is real, not just lore.

Home is for the young, the old,

The weak and the bold.

Home does its duty without being told.

Home is a great listener; it makes no requests.

Home is no conquest.

Home never tells lies;

Unlike a person, home never sighs.

Home, given time, depreciates.

Home is something everybody appreciates.

Home is where the heart grows ever fonder.

Home is where the thinkers ponder.

Home is where we may spend a year.

A decade. A lifetime.

Home completes every verse, every rhyme.

Home never runs out of words.

Home's comfort is poetic;

Its destruction is painful; it is chaotic.

Home provides a perfect safety net;

Home is your best bet.

Home can be filled with meaningless goods and treasure;

Home provides an abundance of joy and leisure.

At home, we're always the first in line;

We feel fine.

We're never told to wait.

At home we're never too early,

Never too late.

Home is something no one can hate.

Home is where love can dwell.

Home is where hopes swell.

Home provides instant relief.

189

Home is at the heart of every principle, every belief.

Home is grand;

It has no brand.

After flying for so long, home is where one can finally land.

Home lights up the street.

It is every artist's retreat.

Home is a personal success.

It holds excess.

Home has a roaring personality; it is not to be tamed.

Home is far better than fame.

Every journey takes us home,

Be it China or Rome.

Home cannot leave us behind.

When we go on for vacation, home waits patiently.

It doesn't seem to mind.

Home can be high or low.

Home is never fast, never slow.

Home is something we all hold close to our heart.

Home is sweeter than a tart.

Home is forever.

It betrays never.

Home is unique and irreplaceable – to get

there one would gladly walk a mile.

One would brave the journey with a smile.

WHERE I BELONG ...

I do not own these woods.

Yet I am forever welcome in the embrace of these trees.

My worry leaves me. It flees!

I walk; I run.

Things are so simple. I look up and find the sun.

It shines down on me, unbridled and alive.

It brings this forest to life.

Days ... weeks ... time has no meaning here.

In the dark, the woods are something to fear.

It is the dark where shadows come out to play.

They fear the light of day.

They have nothing to hear, nothing to say.

They don't get to stay.

These trees grow old; they wither and die.

This forest is pure in its honesty. It doesn't lie.

I begin my walk with a sigh.

As much as I love this place, I do not belong.

I wish to leave as much as I wish to stay.

I want to face the night, chase the day.

This world is beautiful in its intricacies.

It is difficult to choose,

Much as it is difficult to lose.

Every once in a while, we get a choice.

We get to have a voice.

Sometimes we choose wrong.

We forget where we belong.

I watch the stars watch me from afar.

I wonder if I've come too far?

These woods feel warm yet leave me cold.

I must leave this place, escape its hold.

The broken leaves follow me as I go with the wind;

I am not alone.

The chill is finally leaving my flesh, my bone.

The world waits as I make my way home.

About the Author

The author firmly believes in establishing the light that lies in wait at the end of every dark tunnel. It is this light that breathes life into our hopes and aspirations, giving our lives meaning and direction.

About the Book

Symphonies of Life invites you to greet said light with courage and hope, both of which shine like a beacon within our very souls. Once you begin to believe, the darkness begins to leave. May *Symphonies of Life* guide you to your light!

End Notes

My book may have started out small, but somewhere along the way it took on a life of its own. I hope you, the reader, enjoy reading this as much as I enjoyed writing it.

Symphonies of Life is about obtaining the elusive light that lies in wait at the end of every dark tunnel. May SoL guide you to your light.

With Love,
Eman Abid

Printed in the United States
By Bookmasters